# My Life to Live

# MY LIFE
# TO LIVE

## HOW I BECAME THE QUEEN OF SOAPS
## WHEN MEN RULED THE AIRWAVES

## AGNES NIXON

CROWN ARCHETYPE
NEW YORK

Copyright © 2017 by Agnes Nixon

All rights reserved.
Published in the United States by Crown Archetype, an imprint of the
Crown Publishing Group, a division of Penguin Random House LLC,
New York.
crownpublishing.com

Crown Archetype and colophon is a registered trademark of Penguin
Random House LLC.

Photography credits can be found on page 267.

Library of Congress Cataloging-in-Publication Data
Names: Nixon, Agnes, 1922–2016 author.
Title: My life to live / Agnes Nixon.
Description: First edition. | New York : Crown Archetype, 2017.
Identifiers: LCCN 2016044129 | ISBN 9780451498236 (hardcover)
Subjects: LCSH: Nixon, Agnes, 1922–2016. | Women television writers—
    United States—Biography. | Women television producers and directors—
    United States—Biography.
Classification: LCC PN1992.4.N55 A3 2017 | DDC 812/.54 [B]—dc23
LC record available at https://lccn.loc.gov/2016044129

ISBN 978-0-451-49823-6
Ebook ISBN 978-0-451-49825-0

Printed in the United States of America

Jacket design by Elena Giavaldi
Jacket photographs: (left) Ed Eckstein; (center and right) American
Broadcast Companies, Inc.

10 9 8 7 6 5 4 3 2 1

First Edition

*To All My Children: Cathy, Mary, Bob, and Emily*

*And to Paul and Sarah*

*To All My Grandchildren: Ceara, Kelly, Erin, Amy, Oliver, Rory, Galen, Bobby, Maggie, and Jack*

*And to Matt and Jeff*

*To All My Great-Grandchildren: Faye, Riley, and Emma*

*To All My Great-Grandchildren yet to be*

*To my husband, Bob, without whose support* All My Children *would never have been created*

The great and the least
The weak and the strong
The rich and the poor
In sickness and health
In joy and sorrow
In tragedy and triumph
You are All My Children

Theme from my *All My Children* bible, 1965

# CONTENTS

# FOREWORD

I became an *All My Children* fan when Erica Kane was on her first marriage. In the early seventies when I was doing my variety show, I scheduled my lunch break around the time it would air (because there were no VCRs at the time). Unfortunately, when Friday rolled around, there was no way to watch what was going on in Pine Valley because that was our show day . . . so what did I do? During the question-and-answer segment at the beginning of our taping, I simply asked if anyone in the audience had seen the episode that day and if they could bring me up-to-date. It made for some interesting and often hilarious explanations. I was absolutely thrilled later when Agnes Nixon got in touch to offer me a role! And it was a doozy. I was to be "Verla Grubbs," the illegitimate daughter of a carnival con man and snake charmer, who comes to Pine Valley in search of her biological father. Verla looked and dressed exactly like her name (I'll leave that description to the reader's imagination). I returned as the character a few more times, and loved every minute of it.

I was thrilled once more when Agnes sent me her book, asking me to write the foreword. I read it in one fell swoop. The book includes detailed descriptions of the daytime dramas she created, the casting processes, and so much more, which are fascinating to those of us who were hooked on her fabulous storytelling abilities. Moreover, Agnes's own story is as compelling as those in her dramas. She tells us about her parents' on-again, off-again love/hate relationship, and the effect it had on her as a young child who yearned for a normal, loving home. We live through the heartbreak of her first love. We experience her volatile and erratic relationship with her father (who never believed in her writing talent), which makes us admire her drive to succeed all the more. She found the perfect man, married, and juggled her career while successfully raising four children. But her career wasn't easy to come by. The "glass ceiling" was extremely evident in the days when she tried to break through as a writer, being thwarted at every turn. Of course, we know she won . . . but the story of her ups and downs makes this book a true page-turner.

—Carol Burnett

P.S.: I was as sad and mad as everyone else when *AMC* was canceled. It could've gone on forty-two more years! Agnes, you are a wonder.

# PROLOGUE

The Emmys, 1981. I was sitting in the backstage area in the Waldorf-Astoria grand ballroom, waiting for my cue. I was the recipient of the Trustees Award for excellence in production, and I was greatly disturbed.

My insecurities plagued me: I didn't deserve this award. Voices from the past confirmed my fears. My father: *You, a writer? That's a joke.* The head of Procter & Gamble: *Frankly, Agnes, we just don't think you're a writer.* The director of *The Edge of Night: Sweetie, you don't get how to plot a serial.*

Barbara Walters stepped onstage. The destructive voices increased in volume: *That's a joke; you're not a writer; you don't get it.*

Barbara stepped up to the podium, and the noises in my head subsided. She addressed the tables crowded with bright lights of the industry and a television audience of millions. "This is a very special occasion with the Emmys and the Trustees Award. I will tell you about the big one. The Academy of Television Arts and Sciences Trustees Award recognizes achievement in television so extraordinary that it is rarely presented. Previous winners include General David Sarnoff, William Paley, Leonard Goldenson, and Edward R. Murrow, so you can see what kind of award it is.

"Today marks a number of firsts for this prestigious award. It is the first time it has been presented to someone in the daytime area, it is the first time it has been presented to a writer, and it is the first time in the history of this award that it has been presented to a woman. I feel like saying with you all, 'Right on.'

"The recipient today is the creator of *One Life to Live, All My Children,* and the cocreator of *Search for Tomorrow* and *As the World Turns.* By now you know I can only be talking about Agnes Nixon."

I felt a little push on my shoulder. The backstage manager said, "Agnes, that was your cue. Go join Barbara."

As I walked across the stage through a thunderous standing ovation, the applause mounted. Barbara took my hand and said, "One of your shows has been on the air every weekday for the past thirty years. How did you do it?"

Rather than answering her question directly, I began by thanking the academy for the honor. Then I said, "I honestly don't think I deserve it. But if I do, it's because of all the people through the years who have helped me. My Irish family, around whose hearth I learned as a child to love a story. The late, great Irna Phillips, who gave me my first job and taught me the form of the daytime serial, and that every individual's life has a soap opera in it."

I went on to thank the network executives and the producers, directors, actors, and writers, as well as our wonderful *All My Children* family and especially the viewers. I also acknowledged my children and granddaughter for enriching my life beyond measure. Finally, I thanked my husband, Bob: "Long before the voice of women's lib was heard, a little over thirty years ago, he said to me, 'I understand that writing is an intrinsic part of your life. And of course you can marry me, have children, and also have a career, because I will support and help you.' And he always has."

The entire week that followed was filled with festivities related to my Trustees Award. While I appreciated the speeches and parties, my mind was increasingly occupied by Barbara's question. It was one that I had been asked many times but never really considered—and that I hadn't quite answered onstage.

As I looked back for the first time, I realized that my journey to the stage that night included almost as many twists and turns as the shows I'd created. It was full of joy and heartbreak, mentors who helped me and rivals who tried to stop me, and lots of wonderful friends and colleagues along the way. I wasn't quite ready to answer Barbara's question properly—and I still had the rest of my career in front of me—but I looked forward to the day when I could truly share "how I did it" with friends, family, and all the wonderful fans of my shows. When I did, it would be the story of how I decided, early on, that the life I was given was *my* life to live—and how that determination helped me become a wife, a mother, and, against all odds, a writer.

# My Life to Live

# Chapter 1

# PAPER DOLLS

I was named after my mother—my single, working mother who provided for me while we lived with her parents and sisters at a time when most women didn't work outside of the home. And every time she left for work as a bookkeeper at the Independent Life and Accident Insurance Company, I pitched a fit, inconsolable that she was leaving me behind. Little did I know that I would spend my entire adult life as a working mom. I guess there's just something about hard work that runs in our Irish blood.

My maternal grandfather, Michael Dalton, left County Tipperary at age twelve in 1863. He crossed the ocean alone to live with his eldest sister, Emma, who worked as a domestic helper in New Orleans. When he arrived, he found that Emma had died from yellow fever, which had ravaged the state. The twelve-year-old boy managed to support himself by working at a bakery. When he turned fourteen, he lied, claiming to be sixteen, so he could enlist in the Union Army. His aim was to punish the British (who were allied with the Confederacy), whom he blamed for the great hunger that caused the death of many of his countrymen, including his beloved parents. Given his preoccupation with food, after the war he owned and operated a grocery store to care for and feed his wife and twelve children.

My mother, Agnes, was the eleventh child of the twelve born to Michael and Katherine Dalton. The Irish Catholic couple lived with their children in a spacious apartment over their grocery store in Nashville. As was typical of the time, my grandmother Katherine Ryan Dalton had married at age sixteen, and her three eldest daughters were assigned the care of the new babies. So it was that my mother's sister May, who was eighteen years her senior, reared her. When May married and had three children, Agnes thought of the girls as her younger sisters and spent much of her time at her sister's home.

My mother had a very happy childhood. Most of her time and social life were dictated by her years as an A student at St. Cecilia's Dominican prep school. She went to secretarial school, and after graduation, she worked as a secretary at several insurance companies, eventually becoming a bookkeeper.

My aunt May told me more about my mother's life than my mother ever did. Through her, I learned about my parents' courtship and early marriage. My mother was a beautiful girl with alabaster skin and wavy golden hair that framed her face. According to Aunt May, many young men were infatuated with the beautiful Agnes, but only one interested her: my father, Harry Eckhardt.

Harry's father, Henry, had lived in Nashville and was always partial to it. However, in his early twenties Henry had moved to Chicago to try to find a better job. He was still in love with Nashville and, because he had several brothers residing there, often returned to visit. On one such visit, Aunt Kate's friend Maynie Eckhardt introduced her cousin Harry to Kate's little sister Agnes. My father was instantly infatuated with my mother and began a relentless pursuit that she found flattering. His courtship was very different from the docile wooing of the Southern gentlemen who were attracted to her.

Harry came to Nashville from Chicago for a temporary job and lived with his cousins. Young and brash, my father was full of moneymaking schemes that, according to him, would soon render him a wealthy man. None of my mother's family liked him, and soon after they began dating, Harry became extremely possessive. His professions of love and total devotion seemed to impress my mother, but he was also intensely jealous of any other young men she knew. This caused many arguments, and Aunt May told her that she should break it off. She had such protective feelings for my mother and never felt that Harry could make her happy. She encouraged my mother to see other men who courted her. But Harry was always able to convince Agnes to forgive him for his outbursts.

AFTER TWELVE YEARS of pursuit, she agreed to marry him and moved with him to Chicago. My mother's early letters to my aunt from Chicago conveyed a happy, yet busy, tone. She took a position as secretary to a lawyer, and the marriage seemed felicitous. But after a few months, there was a worrisome change. She became pregnant and wrote that Harry was disappointed at the new responsibility. But she believed he would be overjoyed when the baby arrived.

When I was born, I weighed seven and a half pounds, but three weeks later, I had lost four pounds—more than half my weight. I had pyloric stenosis, a gastric ailment that made me spit up any nourishment I received. In a panic, my mother called Aunt May, who immediately got on a train to Chicago. Fortunately, my mother insisted on taking me to a pediatrician, who prescribed a formula. My health improved, but the same couldn't be said for the state of my parents' marriage. Although my mother tried to hide the discord, Aunt May could hear their arguments through the thin bedroom walls. When May boarded the train back to Nashville, my mother went with her, holding me in her arms. My father's furious attempts to keep us with him had finally fallen on deaf ears.

Back in Nashville, the household consisted of my mother, my grandmother, my grandfather, and my four unmarried aunts—Emma, Catharine, Albertha, and Rose. Out of kindness and concern for me, the three elder sisters decided that, together, they would support us for the first year so that my mother wouldn't have to work. However, it wasn't long before she took a job at the Independent Life and Accident Insurance Company. As my mother dressed for work, I would begin to cry. My whimpers crescendoed into screams until my grandmother entered, hustling Mother out of the room, warning her that she couldn't be late. Grandma would then close the bedroom door to shut out my screams, leaving me in agony until I fell asleep, exhausted.

A dollar store now fills the lot at 713 Russell Street where my grandmother's home once stood, so I can't be sure that the house was as cavernous as it seemed when I first toddled across its wide-planked floors. During my first five years, I became accustomed to my mother's daily departures, but I was still lonely. I was left with my grandma Dalton, but after rearing twelve children of her own, she didn't relish the idea of babysitting another small child. She made sure I was fed lunch, took my cod-liver oil, and had a daily nap, but her exchanges with me were limited to a few aphorisms, such as "Children should be seen and not heard," and "You're eating your white bread now." The latter meant that I was spoiled. As a result of Grandma's pronouncements, I rarely spoke in her presence, and to this day I prefer dark bread to white.

The backyard of the Russell Street home was unusually

large. Deep flower beds were dominated by purple irises, Tennessee's state flower. Tall trees with low-hanging branches offered shade from the relentless summer heat. In the rear, bordering a dirt-and-gravel alley, was the chicken yard. Its occupants furnished eggs all week long, and every Sunday dinner was provided by two hens smothered in dumplings and revoltingly thick gravy.

Saturday was judgment day, with Grandma as the Grim Reaper. I was convinced that the chickens knew when it was Saturday and what Grandma's mission was when she approached the pen. Running in terrified circles, the chickens began a deafening cackle. Grandma used only her hands to accomplish her ghastly task. She grasped an innocent victim by the neck and wrung it around and around until its head came off. Then the body continued to whirl about wildly, seeming to be searching for its missing head. I was appalled but also fascinated by this weekly drama. From the safety of an upstairs window, watching Grandma perform her *danse macabre,* I wondered if one day she'd eliminate me as efficiently as she did those chickens.

After the Saturday massacre, I always sought the comfort of my cherished paper dolls. These were not the conventional paper dolls from a booklet containing clothes to be cut out. The source of my dolls was the daily comics, or "funny papers," which I much preferred to the commercial kind because of their lifelike mobility. Cutting the characters out of the newspaper's small squares was tedious work for a four-year-old who only had dull, blunt-tipped scissors. But I had a lot of time on my hands.

When I was a little older, I devised a complicated filing system for my dolls. I took several of my grandmother's discarded telephone books and began cataloging my dolls by the names

I'd given them. A separate phone book formed a subfile according to the clothes they wore and their physical positions—standing, sitting, walking, and running, even dancing, if the comic-strip artist drew such a figure. Every Sunday, I couldn't wait to start cutting out the characters in the funnies, an activity that would preoccupy me all week long. When my beloved aunt Emma read the comics to me, I didn't find the stories very absorbing. But sometimes she offered what she thought the characters in the strips might do or become, and those ideas caught fire with me.

These characters were my "open sesame" to a special make-believe world. While preparing the stage, my mind was busy planning scenes involving my characters. Plotting their lives gave me a sense of control. They allowed "little Aggie" to believe her life could change as dramatically as the lives of her dolls—like Little Orphan Annie, who had Daddy Warbucks waiting to rescue her from loneliness. My most frequently used characters were the well-known Etta Kett, Moon Mullins, Blondie, Dagwood, Daddy Warbucks, and sometimes Annie. I created one doll whose father went to work but would be gone for four days. I named that doll "me." That doll asked me, "Why don't you have a father?" Then the doll said, "You don't have a father because he doesn't love you."

But my favorite, by far, was Tillie the Toiler. At one point, Fred, my ten-year-old neighbor, mentioned that he had kept the Sunday funnies since he was five and had three years of comics I had never seen. With bated breath I asked him, "Do you have Tillie the Toiler and Etta Kett?" When he said yes, I offered to polish his father's shoes for ten weeks in exchange for his collection. And while polishing away, I came up with some starring roles for Tillie.

In the *Nashville Banner*, Tillie was a working girl like my mother and aunts, but that was where the similarity ended. I much preferred my own scenarios for Tillie to those in the funny papers. To me, Tillie was a young, beautiful career woman determined to get what she wanted, and she proved to be smarter than the men in her life. Yet the men seldom resented her. In fact, very often Tillie became the object of their affections. My star paper doll was a femme fatale who got what she wanted—unlike my mother, who slaved away at a nine-to-five job, largely ignored and unappreciated, and with no men in her life.

Only now do I see that my Tillie was the predecessor of Erica Kane.

# Chapter 2

# THE PROBLEM WITH PERFECTION

Growing up, no one in our house ever said Harry Eckhardt's name. I had intuited what the word *father* implied—and that my life was devoid of one. I didn't feel deprived; I was merely trying to fathom how the situation affected my mother, who was, to me, the most important person in my life. No matter how her lovely smile tried to deny it, I was constantly aware of her unhappiness. We sometimes visited her best friend, Marie, with her husband and four children, who seemed to live in loving unity. On the streetcar ride home, I commented on how busy all those children kept her friend.

Mother smiled and said with a deep yearning in her voice, "Yes, but Marie is very lucky."

From the time I was young, I believed the main reason God put me on Earth was to make my mother happy. When I was five, I learned, by accident, why my efforts were so important. Grandma kept some of her things in a large oak cabinet in her sitting room. While looking for glue to mend my favorite ball gown for Tillie, I discovered a slim photo album wedged between *Lives of the Saints* and *Glories of the Holy Roman Catholic Church*. I took it out, and, to my surprise, there was a picture of my mother, younger and even more beautiful. She wore a Grecian-style, flowing white gown, and her lush golden hair was held by three rows of white satin ribbons. Next to her stood a bland-looking young man. I wondered if this was the man my mother married. Was this my father? I was so absorbed in studying the photographs that I didn't realize Grandma had entered the room.

"Drat! I told myself you might find that," she said. "I should have thrown it away. Good riddance to bad rubbish."

"Is that my father?" I asked.

"More's the pity," she snorted.

Despite her scowl, I couldn't resist asking, "What was he like?"

"Didn't you hear me say he was total rubbish? I told Agnes that she ought to marry Ivoe Carlton. He was smitten with her, a gentle Southern man. I told her, 'All you and Harry do is fight. Ivoe would never raise his voice to you.' Do you know what she said to me?"

I shook my head no.

"She said, 'I'd rather fight than be bored to death.' But I reckon she changed her mind, since she left him when you were only three months old."

Grandma seemed to run out of steam. Tucking the album under her arm, she said, "Well, she can't say I didn't warn her." She was about to leave when Aunt Kate rushed into the room.

"There you are, Mama. Have you heard the news?" she asked.

"What news?" Grandma said. "Why did you leave work so early?"

Aunt Kate replied, "Maynie called me at the office. Henry Eckhardt died last week in Chicago. They sent the body back to Nashville for burial. I came home to take you with me."

"Take me where?" Grandma demanded.

"To the funeral home for the visitation. It's from six to nine. You want to change, don't you?"

"Henry Eckhardt wouldn't have gone to my visitation, and I'm not going to his."

"I must go, Mama. Maynie is my best friend, and Henry was her uncle, and besides, he's little Aggie's grandfather."

I had been told that the elderly man who sometimes stopped by to see me was, indeed, my grandfather. As usual, I took my cue from my mother, to whom her father-in-law meant nothing. However, at the supper table that evening, I found that there was much to learn about the young man I'd seen in the photograph album. Grandma, who'd disliked all Eckhardts from the beginning, commented that, unlike the Daltons, they hadn't always been Southerners.

Aunt Kate said, "But, Mama, don't you remember how nice it was visiting back and forth at each other's houses? Why, that's how Harry met—" She stopped abruptly, realizing she had gone too far. With the lull in conversation, my mother rose, took my hand, and started out of the kitchen. Aunt Emma followed us down the hall.

She put her hand on my mother's shoulder and said, "Agnes, I'd be happy to stay with Aggie while you go."

"Thank you, Emma," my mother replied. "But I'm taking her with me."

Aunt Emma frowned. "Are you sure she should go to the funeral home?"

"Quite sure," said Mother. Her clipped manner made it obvious that there was to be no further discussion.

At the funeral parlor, I was just a bewildered little girl frightened by coming face-to-face with death. My mother handled the introduction to my father well. He, in return, was warm and kind. Later that evening, he persuaded Mother and me to come to the Hermitage Hotel, where he was staying. He was an ideal parent that night. To my delight, in his hotel room, there were toys and pretty dresses for me that he had brought from Chicago.

He also told us about the business he had started after we left him, emphasizing that his motivation was to be worthy of reuniting our family. Harry explained that as a teenager working as an errand boy, he'd dreamed of becoming a doctor. When college, let alone medical school, had proven to be too expensive, he'd taken a full-time job at the mortuary, where he felt the owner made an unjustifiably large profit. Riding in the hearse with the driver had spawned many schemes surrounding the business of death. Years later, my mother told me he wanted to invent an embalming fluid to increase the tranquil appearance of the dearly departed. It was met with little support from the business, especially after a trial mixture exploded in the basement.

To Harry, a nation recovering from a devastating depression presented the perfect opportunity for a unique line of burial garments. America's financially strapped working class was loath to have the family's one good suit interred with the departed. The Perfection Burial Garment Company was the answer. Harry had designed a line of clothes that were appealingly inexpensive, and an opening down the back made it easier for the family member or mortuary dresser. In addition, his low-budget feminine creations were of a soft material in flattering shades, with ruffles and lace around the cuffs and neckline. Despite the ultimate destination of these burial garments and an extreme fear of death (about which I learned later), that night in the hotel with us, Harry spoke of his creations as if they would be featured in the next Broadway show.

His return reservation to Chicago had been for the evening following the burial, but he postponed it for a week and spent time pleading with my mother for a reconciliation. She would never have to work again, he promised, and he would build her a beautiful house in Winnetka. I would be sent to a fine school and meet only the best people; the three of us would be a happy family. He seemed so sincere, and I saw my mother beginning to be persuaded. And why not? Although I was only a child, even I could sense that she still loved him. Why wouldn't she want the life he described? I began to envision the future with lots of friends, pretty clothes, and most of all, a happy mother and father.

Harry had rented a car for the week, and we toured Nashville in it. We fed the ducks in Centennial Park and visited the Grand Ole Opry. On the way to dinner, we passed a toy store that displayed a beautiful life-sized doll. When I admired it, Daddy—as Harry begged me to call him—wanted to buy it for me, but the store was closed.

"Never mind," he said. "I'll get you a better one when we get to Chicago."

We arrived at Klemen's, a popular Nashville restaurant with reputedly the best apple pie in the South. Daddy remembered how much he'd enjoyed the apple pie from other visits. Mother recalled a time when he ate two orders of pie, and they laughed about it. During dinner, Daddy told us he had become friends with many important casket manufacturers and funeral directors around the country in the last few years.

"In business," he said, "it's a major factor to have a pleasing personality. No matter how good your project is, establishing a good relationship with the buyer is what clinches the deal."

As he elaborated on the amazing success his company had achieved, and as the waitress removed our plates, two men passed our table. They nodded pleasantly to my mother, who returned the simple greeting with a smile. When the waitress left, Harry asked who the men were. Mother explained that they owned the insurance company where she worked. Harry quickly pushed his chair back.

"I want to meet them," he said.

When Mother shook her head no, the expression on Harry's face started to change.

"Why not? I'm your husband. Let's go."

"I just told you," Mother said. "They're my bosses. I don't know them personally."

"So we'll get to know them now," he said, and started to stand again. "They would like to meet someone of my stature. Come on."

"Harry, sit down."

"They may be your bosses, but I'm their equal." He stood up.

"Harry, sit down. I'm not going to introduce you."

His face started to redden. "Are you ashamed of me?"

"Of course not. It's just not the proper way to do things."

"You're telling me what's proper?"

"I'm telling you I don't know them that well," she insisted.

"You're lying. What's the real reason?"

"Harry, stop it."

Harry's face got even more choleric. "You're having an affair with one of them, aren't you?"

"Harry!"

"Or maybe you're sleeping with both of them."

My mother was in shock. "Harry, don't talk that way in front of Aggie."

"But you don't deny it, do you?" He rose from the chair, tossing his napkin on the floor. "I'll introduce myself."

My mother grabbed my hand and rushed me out of the restaurant. Harry threw some money on the table and ran after us. The terrible wrangling continued in the car, while I cried in the backseat. Eventually, I must have escaped the awful scene by falling asleep. I awakened to find my mother sitting on the side of my bed, gently rubbing my forehead.

She said, "I'm sorry about last night. He isn't always like that. He was sorry, too. He wants to come over and see you. Is it all right if he comes?" I shook my head in a definitive no and burrowed beneath the blankets.

Two weeks later, my mother received a long white envelope with his heavy black writing on it. She read the letter to herself and put it into her desk drawer. Putting her arm around me, she said, "Aggie, your father has invited us to come to Chicago on our vacation."

When I said no, she asked, "Do you mind not having a father?"

Although I was surprised at the question, as always, I tried to give the answer she wanted. "I like the way things are," I said. But no matter how her smile tried to deny it, her unhappiness was as obvious to me as the blue of her eyes. I was glad we did not go to Chicago because my father made me feel such pain when he was around, and I knew how sad he made my mother feel. I did not see him for four years. Although I wrote him every month because my mother told me to, the only replies I received were from his secretary. She explained that while he enjoyed getting the letters, I must understand that he was too busy with his business to write back.

A few years later, when I was nine years old, my father sued my mother for divorce on grounds of desertion. A family friend who was a lawyer handled it for her. She asked for nothing from Harry except for sole custody of me. In explaining it, she said it was better to have it this way—it meant a clean break with him. Therefore, I was puzzled when she told me that I would have to spend several weeks with Harry in the summertime. I never knew if this request was made through

Harry's lawyer, but I came to wonder if it was a way for her to stay in touch with him.

What I *did* know is that I dreaded those two weeks a year in Chicago. Harry bought me quite a few clothes, which I liked. But as a consequence, I had to listen to his tirades about my mother and his resentment of every member of the Dalton family. Every night we had dinner at Henrici's, a popular spot in the heart of downtown Chicago. Sometimes we were joined by a woman he would introduce as an "old friend."

If we were alone, the main subject was the Daltons, especially Grandma Dalton. My father asked very little about my mother, but he had plenty to say about his dislike of the rest of my family. He ridiculed my grandmother and consigned her to the depths of hell.

"How can you stand to live with that mean old bitch? She's totally insane. They should have locked her up a long time ago. She'd always say to me, 'Don't ye take Agnes out alone in the dark.' Does she still say 'ye' when she means 'you'? Crazy bitch. God, how I hated her."

My father's rants about my grandmother made me feel like I was shriveling inside. I wished my family could get along. It made me think of my mother and how unhappy he had made her. The fact that I couldn't change the situation made me feel like a terrible failure.

The Chicago days fell into a routine. We had a small breakfast, and at ten a.m., we went to the Perfection Burial Garment factory. The women workers at their sewing machines outdid themselves in praising me and sharing their dreams of the day when I would be a partner with my father in running this wonderful business. Most distasteful to me was having to witness the bereaved families who visited the factory to make selections for their beloved.

I was appalled when Father would say to me, "Isn't that wonderful!" meaning they were bringing him new business.

After lunch, he had arranged for some of his staff's children to take me to an afternoon movie. He and I had dinner alone, or were invited to the home of a funeral director who was a good friend of his. This man had grandchildren my age, and my father seemed to think that, inevitably, I would have a meaningful friendship with them.

He would ask me on my way back to his apartment, "Didn't you like them?" and "Wouldn't you like to see them when you come back next year?" But I just shook my head.

I was always happy to get on the train to Nashville and rejoin my mother, who met me at the station. I knew that after dinner, when we were in our shared bedroom, she would ask me what my father did while I was there. Of course she knew about the pretty clothes I would bring home, but I think the purpose of her questions was to find out if he was seeing other women and if anyone else meant anything to him. Early on, I told my mother that he wasn't seeing any other women, but eventually I acknowledged that sometimes a woman joined us for dinner. The way she fawned over me indicated she had a special interest in my father. But I never confided that I realized my mother still had feelings for Harry. I knew how it would make her feel if I did.

# Chapter 3

# GUIDING LIGHTS

My mother continued to be a vital part of my early years, but many other people influenced me as well. I attended a parochial school taught by Dominican nuns for seven years, having skipped from second to third grade. Early in the morning, I waited with the other students for the nuns to arrive and open the doors. Each day, my friend Ruth Ellen and her two brothers were driven to school by her father. The ritual was the same, and their arrival never varied. Ruth Ellen's father got out of the front door and opened the back door to let his children out, giving each of them an affectionate kiss and a big hug. *This,* I thought, *is what a father does.* I knew it was the one thing absent in my life, but I also grew to realize I had something very special that other children did not have. I had my aunt Emma.

Emma Claire Dalton was born with one leg much shorter than the other. As a child, she had to wear a painful leg brace and, later, a hideous extension shoe. Even so, she walked with a limp her entire life. Yet she never complained, and her main motivation was to make other people happy. Of all my eight aunts, she alone would become a successful businesswoman. Combining sheer determination and a superior intellect, she partnered with two men in a retail paper business, and the proof of my family's affection for her was that none of her sisters resented her success. Rather, they looked up to her as their leader. Whenever some of them were discussing an important situation, one would often say, "Let's ask Emma what she thinks."

Aunt Emma was known throughout Nashville for her keen acumen, but she confided in me that her desire, even when she was in her midforties, was to be a writer. In pursuing that goal, she took several correspondence courses in creative writing, spending long hours working on assignments. She never had anything published, but she had grace and good humor about the time and money spent pursuing her goal.

Every summer, Aunt Emma created a "backyard circus" for me. The planning and work that she expended on this project were mind-boggling. She built an elephant and a giraffe out of papier-mâché, created games with prizes, and served wonderful food with ice cream for dessert. Every Christmas, I received the dress-up clothes she made throughout the year for me to play favorite characters from fairy tales. I would be Goldilocks, Little Red Riding Hood, Cinderella, Rapunzel, or Snow White. Aunt Emma instilled in me the belief that I had value and the right to be whatever I wanted.

Aunt Emma even made a suit for my cousin David so he could be Snow White's favorite dwarf. Much later on, as astonishing as this is, every Christmas my four children eagerly awaited a box of "dress-up" clothes from their beloved great-aunt Emma.

My cousin David has always been like a brother to me. Perhaps it was because his mother, Rose, and mine—the two youngest children of the Dalton clan—were so close. In addition, on March 14, 1933, there was a terrifying tornado, which I was convinced meant the end of the world. The storm blew away David's house, and they lived with us for several months at my grandmother's home. A very special bond developed between us during that time that has continued throughout my entire life.

One of the treasures we shared during those months together was Aunt Emma's stories of our Irish ancestors. Our favorite was the story of our great-grandparents, Grandma Kate's parents, and how they came together from Ireland to America.

Jamie Ryan and Margret (Peggy) Quinlan fell in love as teenagers at one of the forbidden Hedgerow Schools. In 1860, Protestant Great Britain ruled Ireland and was determined to keep the Irish Catholics a subservient population. A cornerstone of its policy was to outlaw schools, which the locals resisted by holding classes in the fields behind tall hedgerows that hid the classes from the British constabulary. Under such duress, Jamie and Peggy dreamed of moving to America, where life had to be easier and sweeter. When Jamie found an ad in the Tipperary newspaper from a munitions maker in the southern US offering free passage for five years of work, he rushed to Peggy with the news. She was just as excited about the prospect of moving to the US. But when they told her parents, they were outraged at the idea. Peggy's father forbade her to ever see Jamie again. What they did next was told to me as the gospel truth by Aunt Emma.

The desperate couple decided to meet at a secret hiding place on the river Shannon. Peggy pretended to dig up a few spoiled potatoes so as not to look suspicious. Jamie came by at a full gallop on a horse he'd borrowed from his brother and grabbed her by the waist, throwing her up onto the saddle with him. They continued on to Westport, where they set sail, never to see her family again.

They were married on the top deck of the ship by the captain. On these boats from Ireland, there were usually more

funerals than marriages, which was why they acquired the nick-
name "coffin ships." But one death was averted when my great-
grandparents came across a five-year-old with a high fever.

Peggy said, "Jamie, can you help her?"

When Jamie placed his palms on the girl's blazing temples,
the heat rushed out. He then placed her back in her mother's
arms. It was the first time those passengers had witnessed
"healing hands," and they spoke of Jamie's gift until the ship
docked in New Orleans.

Jamie and Peggy had settled in Nashville, had been married
for nine years, and had eight children when he was conscripted
by the Confederate Army. This draft was a last-ditch attempt
by an increasingly desperate Confederacy to win the Civil War.
The Union Army had recently won the Battle of Franklin and
had begun entering the breastworks at Nashville on December 1, 1864. It became apparent that the Union Army had high
hopes of ending the war. The week before, a new battalion of
Union soldiers had pitched camp just across the clay road from
the Ryan homestead. When Peggy went to answer a knock on
her door, she was hoping it would be someone with a message
from Jamie. Instead, it was a uniformed Union sergeant.

"Mrs. Ryan?"

"Yes?" Peggy replied.

"I come bringing a message from our major."

"Yes?"

"Tomorrow morning, the major has ordered that we take
your chickens to feed our troops."

"You're taking all of them?"

"We have very hungry troops, Mrs. Ryan. Major wanted
you to know. Good day to you."

And he was gone. Peggy stood thinking and then opened
the door to the last room she and Jamie had added to the house.

"Children, I have to step out of the house for a few minutes. Girls, start the breakfast. I'll be back in a short while." Tying her bonnet under her chin, Peggy crossed the dirt road into the Union encampment and addressed the sentry on duty with an air of authority. "I have to see the major. Which way is his tent?" The sentry pointed to the largest structure and was unable to ask the lady what she wanted before she had already entered the tent. An amazed major stood up at his desk.

"May I help you?"

Peggy said, "Major, I am your neighbor across the road. I just wanted to tell you how pleased I am to have you near us."

"Irish, I presume?"

"Yes. And I've come here to invite you to partake with me and my children in an Irish tea this afternoon. I make very good Irish day-old bread. Shall we say four o'clock?"

"And what is your name?"

"Mrs. James Ryan, Peggy Ryan."

"Four o'clock then."

With a quick curtsy, she exited.

Some of her lovely garden flowers decorated the table, and she used her only set of china plates. When he arrived, she poured him some tea.

The major said, "This morning you said the children would have tea with us."

Peggy replied, "I'll call them now."

As she opened the door, all eight of her children entered. "Oh, my goodness!" the major exclaimed.

To the children, Peggy said, "I promised you a piece of bread today. Come help yourself. Give the baby to me."

The major stepped in and said, "May I cut it for you?" As he sliced a piece of bread for her and the children, the major said, "What a wonderful family."

Peggy said, "Yes, they are. And if you take the chickens away, my children will die."

It was a lovely teatime.

As Peggy walked him to the door, he called to the sentry, "Pass the word to all the men to leave Mrs. Ryan's chickens alone. If they don't, they will meet the same fate that the chickens would have."

When Aunt Emma told us this story, I said, "She was a very strong woman, wasn't she?"

Emma said, "In our world, all the Dalton women had to be strong."


MY INFLUENCES WEREN'T limited to the strong women in my family. I had many wonderful teachers, but certainly the most important was Eleanor Dubuisson, with whom I took private classes after school from second grade through high school graduation. She was the organist for Holy Name Church, but her talents were manifold. She conducted a boys' choir, gave private piano lessons, taught elocution, and wrote many plays for the students, which she also directed and produced. Eleanor told my mother she thought I had great potential and offered to work with me at a very reduced rate.

The first selection I learned as part of Eleanor's class was a recitation of little poems for an adult audience—or, in my case, my mother's friends, who made me feel like a parlor-room parrot. But at least I learned to be at ease in front of a group.

During subsequent lessons, there was no set formal teaching, no classes, and no books to read. We simply talked about the world around us. And in those illuminating conversations, it was impossible for her to resist sharing her lust for life. She made me understand Shakespeare as if he were the most recent hot teenage author, and she acquainted me with the wonders of foreign countries that I yearned to visit.

I loved to read about how throughout history, people's lives were so caught up in tragedy. For instance, I was fascinated that Queen Elizabeth was so envious of and threatened by her cousin Mary, Queen of Scots, that she sentenced her to death by beheading. As Mary walked up to the executioner's block, no one knew that the queen had her beloved dog hidden in her dress. The ax fell, Mary's body went one way and her head rolled another, and her dog ran out from under her skirt to sit by his mistress's severed head.

Eleanor even made me a faithful listener of the Saturday afternoon grand opera broadcast sponsored by the Texaco company. My favorites were *Madama Butterfly* and *La bohème*. I may not have fully appreciated Lily Pons's high C in *Lucia di Lammermoor,* but looking back, perhaps all the operatic drama was preparing me to write the many dramatic scenes in my scripts later in life.

Eleanor's enthusiasm for the arts and literature encouraged me to cultivate my own opinions, even if they contradicted hers. And the best thing about these lessons was that she treated me as an adult.

I spent hours with Eleanor, studying people whose mundane lives could explode into drama. There was a woman who worked under my mother in the bookkeeping department, Hattie McDaniel—not to be confused with the Academy Award–winning actress—who always stopped me for a few words when I arrived at the end of the workday. She often said she wished her daughter, who was twenty-three and married, was still my age. A week later, the newspapers ran the story that Hattie had shot and killed her daughter after learning that her daughter was pregnant. Hattie's reason was "her desire to save her daughter from the pains of childbirth." I spent much time speculating on the bizarre workings of Hattie McDaniel's mind. I was still mulling the possibilities when the jury returned a verdict of "not guilty by reason of insanity."

Long after, I asked my mother, "Was there anything about Hattie McDaniel that made you suspect she might be crazy?"

Her answer never varied. "No. She seemed just as sane as me. Makes you wonder, doesn't it?"

As shocking as Hattie's murder of her daughter was, nothing compared to the words I would hear from someone I thought was a friend. I was about to learn a powerful lesson by being exposed to humanity's baser side. A young man and I had just had a lovely evening at a high school dance. He drove me home, and we were sitting on the front porch when he said, "I just can't wait until Saturday night."

I asked, "What's happening Saturday night?"

Holding up his fists, he said, "I'm gonna get some black on these."

"From where? What do you mean?"

"I'm going down to nigger town and find a couple to beat up. They'll be good and bloody."

I can't remember what I said, but I'll never forget the anticipatory pleasure he took in the coming carnage—and how much it disgusted me. After that, whenever I was on a bus and saw black adults walk past me and many empty seats, only to stand in the crowded "colored section," I would hear his hate-filled words.

I began to realize how deep racial prejudice ran. Some white people clearly enjoyed the suffering of blacks because it increased their feeling of superiority. They believed that the power to inflict pain had been bestowed upon them by divine right.

I became determined to find a way to help free people of their evil attitudes. I would say to myself, "If only they could see how wrong they are." A lifetime later, I tried to do that with the Carla/Clara Gray story on *One Life to Live*.

# Chapter 4

# THE MILLS OF GOD

The summer before my senior year in high school, during my Chicago visit, my father was unusually benevolent. We shopped for beautiful clothes at Marshall Field's, and he even found pretty shoes to fit my narrow feet. There were also a few long days at the Perfection factory. At dinner, he questioned me about my postgraduation plans without his usual dictum that I would eventually run Perfection with him. His interest seemed so genuine that I shared my plans to go to Denver after graduation. There, I would stay with my aunt Mae. I would teach at a parochial school to make enough money to get my degree in the off-hours at the University of Denver. I thought perhaps Harry would offer to pay for my tuition; after all, he was certainly able to afford it. But there was no mention of financial support.

Instead, he simply said, "Well, you've certainly got it all worked out, haven't you?"

I returned home to Grandma Dalton's house after two weeks, and that fall, I received a peculiar phone call. My mother, who happened to be near the hallway phone when it rang, was the one who answered it. As she entered our bedroom, her voice was tense.

"It's for you. Person-to-person." She got into the other twin bed, and I went out into the hall. The call was from my father's secretary, Miss McCabe. Initially I thought he'd been in an accident, but her cheery tone of voice dispelled that possibility. After the pleasantries were over, she got to the point.

"Wouldn't it be fun," she enthused, "to surprise your father by spending most of your Christmas vacation here in Chicago with him?"

Instantly, a vortex of ideas and emotions whirled in my brain. I knew that this was not Miss McCabe's idea but my father's, and it had to mean an offer from him to send me to college. But why hadn't he made the offer earlier, during my visit last summer? When I mentioned it to my mother, I could sense her ambivalence. She wanted me to get a good education, but she was concerned about my father's antipathy toward her and the whole family.

For the past seventeen years, my mother had devoted her life to me. She had lost her position at the insurance company when it went bankrupt and had begun working for an actuary who sold life and real estate insurance. Her income was barely adequate for our needs. A beautiful woman in her early thirties, she adhered strictly to her Roman Catholic faith. This meant that there would never be another man in her life, not even a good male friend with whom she might have an occasional dinner. This void in her social life made me her total focus. I knew what it would cost my mother emotionally to let my father send me to college. Perhaps I was callous to want to do so, or perhaps it was my determination to explore my energy and wishes. She needed only to hear that I was indeed going to Chicago for Christmas vacation. She knew what would follow and said only, "He's won."

Not realizing how deep my father's desire was to hurt my mother, off I went to Chicago. One evening while driving his custom Cadillac, he observed that I had started calling him

"Dad" instead of "Daddy," to which I replied that the latter seemed babyish. He agreed, saying that I was no longer a baby and, indeed, would be graduating soon. Then he dropped the discussion. Another time, he told me about a daughter of a business friend who was graduating from Northwestern, and he added that it was a fine university. But there was no mention of college for me.

I didn't fully understand a comment Harry made to a friend when he described his future plans for me: "It's a good Catholic school that teaches their students to follow their parents' wishes."

Back at the apartment, he walked over to me, waving a brochure. He said, "You'll get a lot better education from this place than from the University of Denver." Tossing the brochure onto the couch where I was sitting, he said, "See if you'd like to go here."

The next morning he awoke early, made his coffee, and sat at the kitchen table waiting for me. When I came over holding the St. Mary's College brochure, he asked, "What do you think? Would you like to go there?"

"It sounds wonderful," I said.

"It is. I went there last week. I met a terrific nun who is saving a place for you. Shall we drive down today? I told her I'd let her know."

"You did all this without telling me?"

He frowned. "Maybe you'll see that I know what's best for you."

"Of course. I'd love to see it. The sisters at St. Cecilia's say there is no better college anywhere."

When I told him that of course I would love to go, he suddenly said, "Something's come up. I have a meeting today.

Let's just consider it decided. You can tell your mother how happy you are to go to St. Mary's."

My mother's loss was somewhat mitigated by the fact that I would be going to the top women's Catholic college and that I would be home for vacations. When we got an invitation to attend a reception for new students and parents, to my surprise, Harry thought that both he and my mother should attend. My mother readily agreed.

The question foremost in my mind was, would they ruin my first day at St. Mary's? Their monumental arguments had not ended after their divorce. I was terrified that some minor disagreement would escalate into another dreadful episode. As the day of the event drew closer, my anxiety grew. Although it was Harry's idea, he seemed displeased that Mother agreed to come. They must have argued, as I heard her on the telephone one night saying, "Harry, I am coming no matter what you say or do, and that's final! Good-bye!"

For the trip, she bought a black cashmere wool suit with black satin strips on the collar and cuffs. She looked particularly beautiful, and much younger than her age. When I complimented the suit, she replied only, "It cost too much money that I don't have." This made me realize that I wasn't the only person uneasy about attending the reception.

It was a hot September morning in 1939 when Mother and I boarded the L & N sleeper from Nashville to Chicago, where Dad would meet us and take us to South Bend. When we finally walked through the sliding doors at Dearborn Station, Harry gave her an intense stare. But if he thought she was as beautiful as I did, he made no comment. Conversation was minimal on the drive, and as I looked at my parents' somber faces, I wondered what they might be thinking. Then it struck me that they might be as apprehensive about the afternoon as I was. After all, they had now been cast in roles they had never played before—and they would be in a room full of happily married couples. How would they fit in? What would they say? Would they be detected as frauds?

Harry's voice cut into my thoughts. "There it is!"

Looming before us was the imposing but tranquil yellow brick mansion Le Mans Hall, the headquarters of St. Mary's. In a small entryway, upper-class students handed out the name tags of invitees. The last I saw of my parents, they were being introduced to a host of welcoming, smiling couples. I could see that Mother and Dad were actually relaxing and enjoying themselves. The chimes rang at five p.m., signaling the close of the reception. My parents were as demonstrative and loving as any of the other couples, and my relief at their change in mood was palpable. Then Sister Mary Edward tapped me on the shoulder and introduced herself, saying she would be my theology professor. "I had a lovely chat with your mother and father, Agnes. They are so charming. You are a very lucky girl to belong to such a wonderful family."

Everyone else who met them was equally enchanted. For the first time that afternoon, I realized what I had to face—explaining to Sister Mary Edward and the rest of my new world here that no matter what connubial bliss my parents presented, they had been divorced for almost ten years. Under her benign smile, I realized that postponing the inevitable would only prolong my dread.

"I have something to tell you about my parents, Sister."

"I'd be happy to hear it, dear."

I began to tell the truth: "Well, you see, my parents—" I was stopped by a nun who apologized for interrupting.

"Excuse me, Sister Mary Edward, but I couldn't miss this opportunity to meet Agnes Eckhardt."

"Quite all right, Sister. Agnes, this is Sister Regina of our records office," said Sister Mary Edward.

"Also freshman class representative," Sister Regina interjected.

"Nice to meet you, Sister Regina," I said.

Sister Regina then complimented me on my class rank and added that my principal said that I was a playwright. I tried playing it down, but Sister Regina was on a roll, telling me that the school held a contest every fall. She wanted me to write a script for the freshman production and told me that Sister Mary Francis of the theater department would be in touch with me. Then she turned to Sister Mary Edward and apologized again for interrupting us.

Sister Mary Edward said, "That's all right, Sister. Agnes was about to tell me something about her parents."

Sister Regina quickly deciphered my discomfort and put her arm around my shoulder. "Agnes, were you going to tell Sister that your parents are divorced?"

She explained that when the parents of a student had separate living addresses, it was the records department's responsibility to find out the nature of their marital status.

"But, my dear, you must not feel that it will have any effect on you here at St. Mary's."

"Indeed not," Sister Mary Edward said reassuringly.

I was already feeling the warmth that embodied the school. After unpacking and settling into my room, I wrote a letter to each of my parents, saying how much the afternoon had meant to me and noting that they also seemed to enjoy it. Wishful thoughts streamed into my mind, but I kept reminding myself that their reuniting was highly unlikely, even though it was apparent that my parents continued to be in touch with each other.

And then came the weekend of Halloween.

On the church calendar, Halloween was listed as All Saints' Day, with classes canceled the next day. That meant I would be spending the long weekend in Chicago with my father. The morning after my arrival, as my father left the apartment for the factory, he said he didn't have the door key, and thus I would have to let him in when he came back. Later that day, when I opened the door—I thought, for my father—I was hit with a wave of joy. Next to him stood my mother, whom Harry had brought to Chicago as a surprise, to spend the weekend with us.

It was a glorious weekend, and it was impossible for me not to fantasize about a rapprochement. Harry was even civil when speaking about Grandma Dalton.

In a brief moment that my mother and I shared, I said to her, "You two are getting along so well, aren't you?"

A gentle smile lit her face as she said, "Yes, we really are." With an almost girlish confidentiality, she quietly asked, "Should I remarry him?"

I joyfully approved and gave her a big hug. Almost as in one of my trite plays, Harry announced that a new customer had invited him to a garden party in Winnetka the Sunday after Thanksgiving and that he wanted Mother to go with him. She was reluctant at first, claiming that she wouldn't know anyone. But I joined Dad in assuring her that her Southern charm would make everyone her friend. I was preparing myself for a new beginning, but in fact, it was the exact opposite.

The plan was that I would return to the apartment and wait for them to join me after the Winnetka party. When the telephone rang, I hoped they were calling with news too good to save until they saw me. Instead, it was my mother calling from the L & N station, where she was preparing to board a coach car back to Nashville. Her voice was calm and controlled as she said, "It's all over." I knew she was devastated and reluctant to go into detail, so I got only a fragmentary idea of what had happened.

Knowing how alcohol affected him, Harry usually drank very little. When he was with a group of jovial men whom he wished to impress, things often turned ugly. Apparently, this was what happened in Winnetka. When Mother tried quietly to suggest that Harry curb his drinking, he turned on her in a rage. The embarrassing scene was interrupted by the host, who managed to sober Harry up a bit but failed to lessen his fury at my mother. While driving her to the train station, which he insisted on doing, he railed at her for following her "shanty Irish" family's command to leave him and steal his child away from him.

Our call was interrupted by Harry's abrupt entrance.

"That's your mother, isn't it? Hang up the phone! Did you hear me? Hang up the phone, I said!"

When I didn't comply, he grabbed the phone from my hand and slammed it into the receiver. At that moment, I lost it. Although a tiny rational part of my brain was warning me, I plunged on. How insensitive, crass, and brutally selfish he was to inflict such pain on my mother! Letting her think he cared for her, when his goal was to make her suffer!

During my tearful harangue, Harry's face was implacable. Then he picked up the telephone and dialed St. Mary's office, saying that I wasn't feeling well and that he would take me straight to the infirmary on my return.

I protested that I wasn't sick, but he said, "If I say you're sick, you are. We'll leave in a half hour for South Bend. Be ready!"

When I arrived, the nurse assured me that I was quite all right and would be dismissed from the infirmary in about an hour. Why I couldn't leave promptly, she did not explain. When I saw Sister Kathryn Marie standing in the doorway, the answer to my question started falling into place, and I understood why I had to stay for "about an hour." My father had obviously asked for a meeting with the dean of students.

"Katie May," as we affectionately called her, was the stellar being in charge of two hundred young women. When she was lecturing on any subject related to the problems of life, she claimed that thoughtless actions tended to boomerang on the perpetrator. Her most-used phrase was "The mills of God grind exceedingly slow, but they grind exceedingly fine." This phrase has replayed in my mind throughout my life.

Sister Katie said she'd heard I'd arrived and decided to stop by. She added, "We haven't had a visit in a long time, have we? How is your freshman year going?" She was glad to hear that I loved St. Mary's, and then she casually asked, "Tell me, Agnes, would it be correct to say that your relationship with your father is sometimes difficult for you?"

Sister Katie let my tears flow as if she had nothing else to do for the entire day than to spend it with me. From her, I learned that Harry had had me held in the infirmary for an hour so that he could plead for help with his beloved but recalcitrant daughter, whose mother was trying to destroy his relationship with his child. After my own hour with Katie Mae, I felt able to follow her advice to rise above my father's attempts to control my very existence. Harry never again mentioned my mother or my criticism of him, nor did I.

Unselfishly, all Mother said was, "Aggie, I've recovered, so stop worrying about me. Go on with your life, and remember that I'm your biggest supporter."

I immersed myself in St. Mary's after losing the play contest to a member of the senior class. My new goal was to win the following year's contest with a one-act adaptation of Edith Wharton's novella *The Old Maid*. In the same month, it was announced that Catholic University was offering a summer drama scholarship to undergraduates. Father Gilbert Hartke, a Dominican priest (who was a child star in *Our Gang,* a comedy series filmed in Hollywood), was touring colleges and auditioning students for the scholarship. Unable to resist, I tried out. The scholarship was awarded to me for six weeks in the summer. I had to ask my father for his permission to accept, since it involved the cost of traveling to Washington, DC, and living expenses.

"Okay, but don't get any ideas in your head about being an actress. I have other plans for you," he said.

I certainly had not forgotten what he had said about my Perfection career, but hoping things might have changed, I asked, "What plans?"

He replied with total assurance, "You're going to run my business, so forget your mother's ideas. I can just imagine the fool dreams she put in your head when you told her about this cockamamie scholarship."

"Dad, I haven't even told Mother about it yet."

"When you do tell her, be sure to say I have plans for your future. And they have nothing to do with being an actress."

I followed Sister Kathryn Marie's advice to avoid any confrontation with my father. I knew it would have been useless to argue with him, and so I didn't worry about it.

Actually, I didn't worry much about anything at that point, because something had happened that eclipsed my fear of my father, and even worrying about my mother. I had fallen in love.

# Chapter 5

# THE PROMISE OF A KISS

No tea was served at the Sunday afternoon tea dance; its purpose was simply to provide a weekend gathering spot for St. Mary's students and any men from the golden-domed University of Notre Dame who cared to cross the highway. I had been to the tea dance several times since Christmas vacation but decided to finish a term paper instead one afternoon. My next-door neighbor, Jenny, appeared in my doorway, reminding me that, several days earlier, I had promised to go with her. I quickly changed from slacks to a dress my father had bought me.

Actually, there was nothing in my closet that had not been bought by my father, who informed me when he was supplying me with my wardrobe, "Your taste is all in your mouth." At the time, this was the ultimate put-down. Fortunately, his taste wasn't too bad, even though he only designed dresses for women who couldn't complain.

Entering the rec room, Jenny and I passed two young men standing by the window seat. One was very tall, and the other wore a red tie. As I was dancing with a fellow whom I had met at the sophomore cotillion, the red tie cut in on us and said, "My name is Jim Purcell, but I'm not the one who wants to dance with you. It's that guy over there. Come on."

With that, he led me to the tall one and introduced him as

Hank Priester. As Hank took my hand and started trying to move with the music, he said to me, "You look just like my little sister." Not exactly what a young woman wants to hear!

He told me that he was the first of seven children—five boys, followed by two girls. I identified myself as being an only child and said that I was envious of his large family. (I omitted the fact that my parents were divorced.) While we danced to several other numbers, Hank continued to talk about his family, and then it was time for the dance to come to a close. It was only when the two boys left that I realized that Hank was the most handsome young man I had ever met. But I thought that I would probably never see him again.

So I was surprised when, on the following Monday evening, Hank called to say he and Jim would like to take me to a movie and dinner afterward on Friday evening. Thinking that this was a bit weird, I accepted, but wondered which of the two was my date. Hank clearly was not at ease in my company, as he kept assuring me that Jim would soon join us. In fact, he spent most of the main feature walking up and down the corridor, yelling, "Yo, Jim! Jim, yo!" clearly disconcerted when he got no response. Meanwhile, I was thinking that he was very good-looking, but his looks were equaled by the strangeness of his personality.

For dinner we went to the popular Rosie's Pizza Palace, where there were many other students but no Jim. By now, Hank did not seem overly concerned about his missing friend. He spent the first few minutes talking about his family, which led him to share that religion was a big bone of contention between his parents—his mother was a devout Catholic and his father a staunch atheist. The ease with which Hank talked about his parents' differences was infectious, because I found myself able to tell him that my parents were divorced.

As we sat over our bowls of Rosie's spaghetti and talked freely about our own lives, I felt as if Hank were an old friend.

When the waiter brought extra sauce for the spaghetti, Hank remarked, "I guess Jim decided to stand us up."

By the time the dessert was served, Jim Purcell was definitely irrelevant. Eager to know each other's family history, we began talking about our maternal grandfathers, who were both Irish, and whom each family considered its cornerstone—and the source of its inner strength.

When we got back to St. Mary's, two of my friends were waiting to say hello to Hank. After I said good night to Hank they immediately followed me up to my room.

They thought he was a dreamboat and were full of questions.

"Was it fun? What movie did you see? Did that Jim guy really go with you?"

Then Jenny took over. "Let's get to it. Is he a good kisser?"

"Yes, right. Tell us. Did you like it?" Loretta asked.

Feeling inadequate, I said, "Nothing happened. He didn't kiss me."

"You've got to be kidding!"

Knowing they wouldn't understand, I replied, "He's very shy. But he did invite me to the prom tomorrow night."

"He didn't already have a date?" Loretta asked in amazement.

"Obviously not," I replied. "He told me he doesn't like to go to dances."

"So let's get back to the kiss," Jenny said. "After the prom."

"Or before," Loretta suggested.

While getting into my bed, I realized how much I had wanted Hank to kiss me and wondered if he ever would.

The next night, the prom hall was beautifully decorated with spring flowers. When Hank opened the taxi door for me,

he looked incredibly handsome in his formal suit. He complimented me on my dress, but still my insecurity continued to
mount. Would he kiss me tonight or not?

Some of Hank's friends who lived in his dorm were there
with dates and suggested to Hank that we should swap part-
ners. I would have been happy to remain dancing with Hank,
but I went along with it. Hank and I switched with Jim and
his date. When we were dancing, Jim said, "Hank has been a
no-date dude as long as we've known him. But things changed
after he danced with you that afternoon at St. Mary's."

"He only danced with me because I looked like his little
sister," I replied.

Jim laughed. "That, and a thousand other reasons. Give
him a little time, okay?"

Then he walked me back to Hank and his own date. After
the prom, as we started to get into the taxi, I was hopeful, but
I had to shake my head no when I saw Jenny and Loretta waiting for me.

"He just held your hand?" asked Jenny. "What's his
problem?"

"He's into sports," I said. "He talked about them the whole
time in the cab."

"What's kissing got to do with sports?" Jenny asked.

"Take my advice. Dump him, tomorrow afternoon," said
Loretta.

I said, "I can't."

"Why not? Are you afraid you'll hurt his feelings?" asked
Jenny.

"It's something else." In a very quiet voice I admitted, "I'm
in love with him."

Loretta said, "What? You just met him on Sunday; are you
kidding?"

"I've never been so serious about anything in my life."

The next day Hank invited me to watch him run in a Sunday intramural track meet. Before the meet, Hank put his watch in my purse, saying that he would get it after he had showered and dressed. Transfixed, I watched as the young men with such beautiful bodies, grace, and motion circled the track below me. As I watched Hank seemingly float around the ring, I could see why he loved it.

After the meet, we drove to the lake for a deli picnic. We spread out some blankets on the bank of the lake. He said, "What did you think?"

"I loved it. You seemed to be floating."

"That's why I love it so much. When I'm racing, I feel so free. Like my body is flying around the top of the world. I am Hermes."

"Who?"

Hank said, "Hermes, the Greek god of the Olympics. I think you were sort of shocked when I told you I had his winged foot tattooed on my arm."

"I get it now. By the way, Hermes, here's your watch." As I handed him the watch and he started putting it on, I saw that he'd left something else in my purse.

"Hank, you left your class ring." I took it out and offered it to him.

"That's for you," he said.

"What do you mean, for me?" I asked.

"I want you to wear it all the time. We'll have it cut down to fit you." His words suddenly gave me the strength to tell him what I really wanted to say.

"But, Hank, you haven't even told me you love me."

He took my hand and said, "Well, I love you so much. Now you say it."

"Okay," I said. He took my hand and smiled. I said quietly, but honestly, "I love you, Hank."

He said, "There's something else that I haven't done yet."

"I know."

"But I sure have been thinking about it."

Then he took me in his arms, and the picnic supper by the lakeside was on hold for quite a while.

As we drove back to St. Mary's, both of us in a glorious glow, Hank said that he had told his parents he was in love with me. I told him that I'd spoken to my parents about him, too, but I had been waiting for a sign that he felt the same way. Hank laughed, and since we were at a red light, we kissed again.

After saying good-bye to Hank and affirming our plans for the coming weekend, I went to sign the hour of my return—as students were required to do—and found a message saying that I should call my father immediately and that it was very important. I wondered what could be so important to talk about at that time of the day. The answer to that gave new meaning to the word *shocking*.

Harry answered the phone, and I said, "Dad, you wanted me to call you?"

"What took you so long?"

"It's—" As often was the case, his sentence cut off the end of mine.

"Were you out with what's-his-name?"

"His name is Hank, and yes, I was with him."

"Listen! His family is rich. I mean, really rich! Do you get it?"

"Get what?"

"I want you to do anything you can to marry him."

"What?"

"Don't you understand what I'm saying? Tell me you understand."

Appalled, I said, "I guess I do. But why do you want that?"

"Because I want to be in with that family. They will give me the help I need."

"What do you need?"

His tone implied that if there were a list of imbeciles, I would be at the top. "I want my business to grow, to be nationwide. I need to be in with those big guns and follow them into the market."

"What market?"

"Don't play dumb with me. The stock market. Those fellows get tips that pay off in the millions."

"You want the Perfection Burial Garment Company to be nationwide?"

"I'm not that stupid. I just want to expand into other products. For instance, lingerie. Maybe you don't know, but I'm having dinner this coming Tuesday night with Hank's parents."

"What? Why?" I asked, aghast.

"Because they called and invited me. They got a letter from their son about you. That's why I know if you play your cards right, everything will work out."

I was so horrified that my flesh was crawling. I tried to refuse his awful plan, but he cut me off.

"Listen, I wasn't born yesterday. I intend to impress them. I'm a good salesman. I make people like me. They'll be glad when I'm Hank's father-in-law. I'll do my part; just be sure you understand yours. Talk to you later."

With that, he hung up the phone, cutting me off. I sat staring at the phone, dumbfounded, until Loretta, who had come up behind me, spoke. "What's happened? Come on! Tell me what happened. Did he . . . ?"

Still distressed from the phone call, I nodded my head. "Yes, he kissed me."

Puzzled, Loretta said, "You don't look very happy about it."

"It was wonderful, but I'm so tired."

I bade Loretta good night and went up to my room. I got into bed, but as exhausted as I was, I couldn't sleep. I was terrified that Harry was going to have dinner with the Priesters. How awful would it be?

# Chapter 6

# THE EIGHTH CHILD

Since it was the week of exams, Hank and I didn't see each other until Friday, although we talked on the phone often. But early Wednesday morning, he called to say that his parents had called him from their room at the University Club, saying how impressed they were with my father. They thought he was delightful, and fortunately, he shared their political outlook (which meant that he adamantly opposed the war and was an ardent Republican).

Naturally, I was relieved that my father had made a good impression on the parents of the man I loved—especially when Hank told me they wanted me to visit them in Davenport, Iowa, that summer, after I finished my six-week theater scholarship at Catholic University in Washington, DC.

As soon as I hung up with Hank, the phone rang. It was Harry. His opening salvo was, "I don't know how you got it so wrong. Those people don't have big money; it's her brother who has all the money and the business, the Walsh Construction Company."

"Dad, I never said—"

He continued. "And you were ready to throw yourself at that boy. Ready to get pregnant."

"I never said that! You told me—"

"Well, you'd just better be thankful that I called Dun and

Bradstreet and found out the truth. I got a little suspicious when she started talking about her brother and his construction company. You need to marry money, so don't let that boy have his way with you. Understand?"

Knowing the futility of trying to set the record straight, I just said, "I understand, Dad."

My six weeks at Catholic University were exciting and stimulating, but my upcoming trip to Davenport to visit Hank's parents preoccupied my mind. Still, my scholarship was a terrific learning experience for which I was very grateful. I'd won my scholarship on the basis of an acting audition, which made me toy with the idea of being an actress, but I also took a playwriting course from a talented director and playwright named Walter Kerr. (Kerr, of course, would go on to an illustrious career on Broadway and even have a theater named for him.)

Professor Kerr's lecture about coming up with the idea for a play was spellbinding. It impressed me so much that I began thinking about writing instead of acting. As he spoke of his conviction about being a writer, I felt as if he were talking only to me. He said that no matter whether you were describing the major character or a minor one, you had to be able to *become* each character—to know how they thought and what motivated them throughout their lives, for good or bad. "When you know them as well as you know yourself," he said, "you'll be able to make them come alive." In years to come, I would often credit that advice for illuminating what it means to be a writer. I will always thank him for showing me the way.

During the summer theater in DC, Professor Kerr directed one play, *Hotel Universe* by Philip Barry. The female lead was Julie Hayden, and the male lead was a young actor just getting started on Broadway, Hugh Franklin. (In a nice twist of fate, Hugh would wind up playing Dr. Charles Tyler on *All My*

*Children* from its premiere show in January 1970.) The other parts of the play were filled by students from the acting class, and I was fortunate enough to be offered a part on the condition that I dye my hair dark to prevent there being another blonde onstage with Miss Hayden. I agreed to it, although I made sure that I could wash out the vegetable dye before going to Davenport. In my first acting role at Catholic University I felt something akin to stage fright, but that condition was nothing compared to my apprehension about visiting Hank's parents the following week.

I rode the Rock Island Rocket out of Chicago on an early August afternoon. Two hours later, I heard a click-clack on the train's speaker system, and the conductor's voice rasped out, "Davenport, Iowa, next stop."

Looking out the window, I saw Hank standing on the platform; he saw me, and even before the train had come to a full stop, he jumped into the car, grabbed me in his arms, and carried me to the platform. The conductor reprimanded us and handed Hank my luggage. The Priesters' house at 1800 East River Drive was a large red-brick colonial on a high hill overlooking the great Mississippi River. It had too many rooms to count, but above all, it exuded life and joy. Hank's parents were charming and obviously well educated, and they immediately eased my anxiety. And despite my father's comments about their financial state, they were far from paupers. As Hank told me about growing up in this gracious and happy home, I was struck by how different it was from where I grew up. Although I felt like the luckiest person in the world to be welcomed into this loving family, I also realized, with a bit of sadness, just how lonely my own childhood had been.

The house had six bedrooms, a spacious parlor, a dining room, and a music room with a self-contained pipe organ, an electronic piano, and a Steinway grand. The lush front lawn swept down to the banks of the river. The beautiful backyard was more than an acre. Preparations were under way for a cookout arranged for Hank's friends and siblings. Conversation around the picnic table was about the possibility of war and which branch of service these young men, all under age twenty-five, would be in. Hank's father, Henry—or "Pop," as the kids called him—was a staunch member of America First and passionately opposed to the US entering the war. He seemed to be getting very fidgety as the young men continued to talk about the various armed services, and possibly having lost patience with such talk, he slowly rose from his seat and headed toward the house. Everyone else also rose and followed him into the music room.

Hank had told me about his father's musical talent, but I soon learned that his artistry was unrivaled in the area. *Genius* was the only word to describe him that evening. He played the great masterworks for his own pleasure and filled the house with music. Yet when anyone called out the title of a popular tune, Henry would simply ask the person to hum it. With his sheer versatility, he would start playing the piece with all the musical twists and blandishments, calling upon the group to sing along. His talent was so extraordinary that I was left with only one question: How could this man of such musical ability bear to spend his workdays in financial investments?

Toward the end of the evening, Hank's little sisters, Eda and Kiki, returned from their summer sleepover camp. Even I could see the resemblance between Eda and myself. The two little girls were adorable and polite.

The following autumn, when we were both back in college, Hank and I returned to Davenport for the weekend whenever possible, and I came to think of 1800 East River Drive as home. There were many good times in that comfortable red-brick house, all of which I enjoyed, from the Ping-Pong tournaments to the summer nights when it was warm enough for all the children—all eight of us—to sleep on the summer porch. But what I most enjoyed was what seemed most typical of that wonderful time of my life: the dinner hour.

With seven children and their devoted parents treating me as if I were the eighth child, I found the joy of family that I had never experienced. I loved everything about it, from discussing their heated sports events to their teasing me as I tried to master eating an artichoke. My determination to be a writer notwithstanding, I knew that I also wanted to be the mother of a close-knit family. Hank agreed, but added that he suspected having seven children was a bit excessive.

Hank took me into the countryside to see his special places for fishing and hunting. He reminisced about how his father took him and his brothers on long-remembered outings, and how he would like to take his own children on similar excursions. I told him how much it meant to me to be a part of his family, and that I hoped we would have a family like his. The day was breathlessly beautiful—the sky so blue, the air so fresh and crisp. We knew that our love would go on forever.

Hank suggested we get engaged and be married at Christmas. I told him that if we got married, my father wouldn't want me to continue college but would rather I go into his business, and that he might also want Hank to be part of it. Hank understood, and we decided to wait until all the talk of possible war was over. Then we would have a long engagement and a beautiful wedding. I told him that the class ring on my finger meant as much to me as a diamond would. We agreed not to do anything impulsive and to anticipate the future with nothing but joy.

# Chapter 7

# LIEUTENANT PRIESTER

As the church calendar afforded us another holiday on December 8, we decided to go back and celebrate my birthday a few days early in Davenport. Knowing that Hank's father vehemently opposed the war, there was an unspoken agreement among us to avoid the subject. Hank's mother, Katie, mentioned that the radio listings showed that Lynn Fontanne would be reading a new poem entitled "The White Cliffs" by Alice Duer Miller. She looked at her watch and said, "It should be starting right now. Let's turn on the set." Henry went to the radio and turned to the station, and we settled down to enjoy Fontanne's melodious voice.

Right in the middle of the poem, her voice was cut off: "We interrupt this program to bring you a special announcement," the announcer said. "The American base at Pearl Harbor in the state of Hawaii has been attacked by the Japanese army." Everyone was quiet, and then Pop purposefully turned the radio dial, cutting off the announcer's voice. After that, we were draped in silence until Hank's mom spoke. "Henry, I think you should drive these young people to Chicago tomorrow. We should all stay close."

Along with the rest of America, we were in shock from the Sunday morning sneak attack. During such uncertain times, rather than take the train from Davenport, Pop would drive us to Chicago to catch the South Bend train, which we would then take back to school. On that long ride, Hank and I held hands and listened to President Roosevelt over the radio.

Without having to say so, we knew our thoughts were the same. Our future, which we had just discussed late into the previous night, was about to change. As much as we wanted to marry, there were many reasons not to. Hank was all for my pursuing a career as a writer, which meant I should finish my schooling. We knew my father would not pay for my continued education if we were married and that Hank would need a job of his own.

Both of us felt that my father's rather surprising acceptance of Hank as his future son-in-law was greatly influenced by his idea that Hank would help persuade me to take over Perfection Burial Garment. Hank was a junior at Notre Dame at this time and was primed for the draft. December 7 had changed our fates, along with the fates of many others.

When Hank's father had heard the news of Pearl Harbor, he knew his worst fear had come true. His twenty-year-old son would be called up in the draft that had been authorized by Congress two years earlier. Instead, Hank, like six million other young men, decided to enlist, and he volunteered for the air corps right away.

When he told me his plan, my heart sank. Consumed by fear, all I could say was, "Oh Hank, that is so scary."

He said, "Look, Ag, I will come back to you a whole man or not at all."

THE FOLLOWING WEEKS were filled with the details of Hank's enlistment in the army air corps and my transfer to Northwestern University for the winter semester. I wanted to transfer because St. Mary's only had basic liberal arts courses, whereas Northwestern had writing and acting classes.

My father agreed to the transfer on one condition. "Understand that you are taking liberal arts courses—not this speech school stuff about being a writer."

He was against anything having to do with the entertainment business and thought that the liberal arts were what people took to go into business. He didn't think I would need any business courses because he was sure he could teach me anything I'd need to know. I knew he would teach me by controlling me.

The new fall term at Northwestern was busy and exhausting, but at least it kept my mind from the ache of missing Hank. However, I made the mistake of thinking that by taking a liberal arts course, I would be able to spend some time in the School of Speech, auditing interesting classes and benefiting from its extracurricular activities. In reality, my liberal arts schedule left me no free time.

That spring, I waited for letters and phone calls from Tulare, California, where Hank was stationed for flight training. I returned home to Nashville and got a job to save enough money to visit him in California at the end of the summer, a trip during which we planned out what our lives would be like when he returned.

Shortly after my visit, Hank got the orders that he was shipping out to a remote air base in Alaska's Aleutian Islands, a long strand of islands stretching from the Alaskan mainland into the Pacific Ocean to within fifty miles of Russia. As it turns out, the base, on the island of Attu, had a complex history, which I didn't know at the time.

A year before, on June 3, 1942, a small Japanese force had begun an invasion of the Aleutian Islands—during which they would overrun Attu—in hopes that seizing control would prevent an American attack on Japan from the northern Pacific. The very next day the imperial navy had launched a massive assault on Midway Atoll to capture our crucial airfield and harbor halfway between the American mainland and Japan. The odds would have been very much against the US, save for a tremendous breakthrough. We had just cracked the Japanese code and Admiral Nimitz had their complete order of battle. The admiral had devised an audacious trap that both our men on the ships and our pilots, who sank four Japanese aircraft carriers and shot down many of their seasoned pilots, executed beautifully. The Battle of Midway was not just the first Allied victory; it was a blow so severe it became the turning point in the war.

The purpose of Japan's successful attack on Attu now seems to have been to draw the American fleet away from Midway, which might have worked but for the code breakers. But Japan's control of Attu was still dangerous, and a year later, the US feared the base would give the Japanese a launching pad for an assault on the mainland. The battle to reclaim Attu was launched on May 11, 1943, and we won it back only following weeks of fighting and a final banzai charge that cost six hundred American lives, more than we lost at Pearl Harbor.

It was against this backdrop that Hank was sent to the newly reclaimed army air corps P-38 fighter base to defend this closest point of America to Japan. He conveyed his location information using a secret code devised by his father, although the censors still shredded his letters. All the pilots were extremely disappointed with their arctic air base, he shared; the action there had been six months ago and they wanted to be at the front in Germany or the South Pacific.

Hank's letters would describe the pilots as sitting around

and playing checkers, bridge, chess, cribbage, poker, or any other card game known to man. He also described the "willa-wawas," the huge clouds of fog that engulfed them and made any possibility of vision and sense of direction impossible. Reading Hank's letters made me worry less, but at night in the school library, I would pore over the atlas of the Pacific and wonder what Hank was not telling me. I could clearly see that the love of my life was the closest American fighter pilot to Japan.

Hank added a postscript at the end of the letter that somehow escaped the censor's scissors: "Just got a message from my cousin Brud Walsh. His ship will be pulling into the Aleutians in a few days, and he would like us to get together for dinner. He will call me when they arrive. Looking forward to seeing him."

The next day, a very brief letter from Hank arrived, which ended with, "Brud just called. We're having dinner tonight, so I have to leave. Will write tomorrow afternoon. Much love, Hank."

As I was putting the remaining scraps of Hank's letter in the envelope, I heard Harry's footsteps outside in the hall. His walk always had a cadence that forecast anger. This time, he had received the semester bill from Northwestern and noted that I had transferred from liberal arts to the School of Speech. According to him, I was an ingrate and lying lowlife, but still nothing could change his mind about my running the business after I graduated. My father was fixated on the thought that my mother was rearing me as she wanted me to be. He was determined that I would be under his command.

Earlier that week, I'd seen a doctor about a persistent pain in my abdomen. The doctor said I needed an appendectomy, and he'd scheduled it for that afternoon at the hospital. As I closed my overnight bag, I realized I actually preferred an operation to hearing any more of Harry's diatribe.

Afterward, I thought about starting a comedy for my next playwriting assignment, but then the mail arrived with a brief letter from Hank, telling me about two pilots who were being transferred to the European theater and who'd received a forty-eight-hour pass to go home. "Wouldn't that be terrific! I guess I don't have a prayer, but I am going to apply for a transfer." From then on, I was living in a fantasy world where Hank was coming home on that forty-eight-hour leave. My fantasy was interrupted one afternoon when my father stopped the car at the factory.

His secretary came out to say, "Mr. Eckhardt, Mr. Priester just called. He wants you to call him back." She gave him Henry's phone number on a slip of paper, and I was back in my fantasy. *Maybe Hank really is coming home,* I thought as I got out of the car and followed my father into his office. He dialed the number and I heard him say, "Hello, Henry. This is Harry. Do you have good news?" I couldn't wait to hear something encouraging. And then suddenly I saw my father's face change. He said, "Oh . . . we'll be in touch later today." I already knew what Henry had said. I fell apart.

"Calm down . . . Calm down. Don't you think I have enough on my mind? Hank is MIA. That's not gonna do you any good. Stop crying. This is terrible! How are you going to find another man who would ever want to marry you?"

My father's cruel words cut into my broken heart. While I had often suffered from his lack of sympathy, his words set a new low. For the first time I realized that he was truly sick or damaged.

I rushed to Davenport. Hank's parents and I could only

embrace one another. We felt heartbreak beyond words. All we had ever heard about MIAs was that they never came home, so we knew a final report would say that he was deceased. The letter that arrived from the War Department was reported in the Davenport newspaper:

> Mr. and Mrs. Henry C. Priester Sr., 1800 River Drive, received official confirmation Friday of the death of their son Lieutenant Henry Priester Jr. in the Aleutian area on Feb. 4, 1944. He was a pilot of a P-38 fighter plane.
>
> According to the letter received by Mr. and Mrs. Priester, Lieutenant Priester took off from an Aleutian air base for a bombing attack on the Paramushiro Naval base. He failed to return. Hope had been held for some time that he might have been forced down on a barren island, but the official word confirmed his death. He is listed as a flyer killed in action. Lieutenant Priester was in his third year at Notre Dame University when he enlisted in the Army Air Corps in February of 1942. He was graduated from the Twin Engine Plane School at Williams Field, Chandler, Arizona, on April 12, 1943, when he was commissioned.

Hank had named his P-38 fighter plane "Kida," combining the last syllables of his two little sisters' names, Kiki and Eda. The most heart-wrenching moment of that awful day was when the girls came home from school.

Eda said, "Did they find him? Because you said he's missing."

Henry answered, "No, darling. I'm afraid they aren't going to find your brother."

Kiki asked, "What happened to him?"

Henry said, "Honey, his commanding officer just let us know he was killed attacking a Japanese air base on the Russian coast. Your brother was very brave."

Kiki and Eda started crying. They rushed to me, and we hugged.

As Hank and Kida had disappeared into the icy waters of the Bering Sea, there was no funeral. Instead, there were church services and memorials. Hank's parents set up a fund for an annual picnic for orphanage children to have a lovely day in memory of their young son who had so loved children.

A few days later, a letter arrived from a fellow fighter pilot describing the dinner they shared on the last night of Hank's life. Here is an excerpt:

Last Wednesday, February 3rd, Hank came aboard for dinner and brought me a case of beer. Hank and I sat around in the skipper's quarters and talked about everything including his mission the next day, with which I was (somewhat) familiar. We knew it was a serious and risky job. It would have been a depressing evening if it hadn't been for Hank's quiet confidence and sense of humor. He didn't underestimate the dangers—in fact, he calmly described them—but it gave you the feeling that he was prepared for anything. When you looked at and talked to him about his business, you thought more about Hirohito's coming trouble than Hank's problems. He certainly didn't exhibit any stupid enthusiasm for the task, nor any reluctance. There was a job to do.

"No beer for me. Tomorrow I make like a bird," I remembered him saying.

Leaving the ship, Hank paused on the gangway and startled me.

He said, very seriously, "Boy, how I wish I had a son."

He meant it, too—though he didn't say exactly why.

I just couldn't tear myself away from the surroundings of Hank's home. I would go down to the basement and look at the Ping-Pong ladder on which he'd handwritten a record of his game with his brothers from the previous summer. I went into his room to see the trophies that he'd won for his track records at Lawrenceville. I remembered telling him that I hoped we would have a son who would go to Lawrenceville. Then I broke down again, wishing I could be with him.

One day, back at school, it got so bad that I walked down to the Lake Michigan shoreline adjacent to the university. I just kept walking and walking, telling myself that I could just walk right into the lake, and then I wouldn't be lonely anymore. While I considered that, I heard my roommate, Felicia, call me. She grabbed me and said, "What are you doing?"

"I'm trying to find Hank."

"Come on. Let's go to the room and talk about him."

I said, "He will never be back."

Felicia got me to our room and made me lie down. She told me that one of my classmates in my script-writing course had a message from the professor that he was still waiting for the final script I had to turn in before the course ended.

I said, "I don't think I can write anything."

Felicia said, "Agnes, yes you can. You have to."

For days, I sat staring at the typewriter. In order to graduate I had to turn in a final script, but in my devastation over Hank, my wellspring had dried up.

The next afternoon, Felicia said, "Agnes, come on, you have to figure out what the subject is for the script you have to turn in."

I said, "I can't think of anything."

She glanced over at a photo of Hank that I'd kept and said, "Hank's picture is looking at you."

The next day, a letter arrived from Eda describing how her mother had gone to mass for Hank with a friend and then to breakfast. While she was gone, Mr. Priester had put away some of Hank's things because seeing them was causing his wife more pain. I sat holding Eda's letter and looking at the wonderful picture of Hank in uniform. In that moment, I knew that making Hank disappear wouldn't make me feel better. Instead, I placed his photo behind my typewriter so that we were looking at each other. Suddenly I put paper in the typewriter and started writing.

In my mind, I was seeing a father surrounded by mementos of his son. The father said that his boy had asked him to keep these things for him until he came home. As the father picked up each item and talked about it, we heard a scene from the boy's life. It wasn't until the end of the script that we learned that his son gave his life for his country. As the father pointed out, there was no fanfare, no medals, no hurrahs, no celebrations—that was why I named it *No Flags Flying*.

My crying kept me from sleeping that night until I handed it in to Professor Hunter the next morning. The next afternoon, I was again drawn to Lake Michigan. I was walking there when Professor Hunter tracked me down.

"Agnes, I want to talk to you about your script."

"I'm sorry I was late getting it in," I said.

"It was really terrific, Agnes. It has universality. You should be very proud of it. And so should he."

Three weeks later, I went to Chicago and spent a little time with Harry.

I told my father about the script and asked if he'd like to read it.

Harry took it and said, "When I have time, but I have something to say to you. You may think I'm being arbitrary, but the truth is, I'm thinking of your own welfare. This writing gimmick won't take you anywhere, but the business will support you for the rest of your life."

But I hadn't given up. Hearing those kind words from Professor Hunter had given me my first glimpse of happiness since Hank was killed. It made me realize that I still wanted to have a writing career. I felt that Hank was somewhere encouraging me to keep going, no matter what my father said.

Another result of my losing Hank was I couldn't bear to be in the company of other young women who had someone they deeply loved and were planning a life with. Unlike them, all I had left from my love for Hank was that he had encouraged me to be a writer. As a matter of fact, when his English professor had assigned the class to write a short story, Hank had said to me, "Ag, you have to help me. I can't write a story. I don't know where to begin."

I'd said, "Let's start with a girl and a boy."

And so I'd written a story for Hank, which he turned in. The next week the professor was complimenting him and said, "Mr. Priester, this is a very good short story, but I think I detect a little feminine influence."

Now my father was asking me how I thought I could crack this silly writing business. I told him that the Writers Guild of America gave out a list of radio programs that would accept scripts on speculation. They wouldn't necessarily pay you, but perhaps someone would like your work and eventually buy a script from you. Harry laughed at this idea, but the next day he asked me, "Do you know a woman named Irna Phillips?"

Of course I knew who she was. Irna Phillips had started the first daytime radio serial. It was called a "soap opera" because its audience was largely female and its sponsors, such as Procter & Gamble, made products used in washing. Harry said that Irna Phillips was a patient of our doctor, and through him, he had set up a meeting for me at ten a.m. the next morning. I was thrilled at the prospect but also suspicious.

I was familiar with "soaps" because, as a child, I had occasionally listened to the work of a soap opera script-writing husband-and-wife team, Frank and Anne Hummert. Chief among the many idiosyncrasies of the Hummerts' style was their use of the same introduction at the beginning of every episode. For example, after announcing the title of *Our Gal Sunday,* the announcer would declaim, "The story that asks the question, can a beautiful young girl from Cold Creek, Colorado, find happiness as the wife of England's richest, most handsome lord, Lord Henry Winthrop?" Or at the beginning of *Portia Faces Life:* "The story which proves that romance need not pass a woman by at thirty-five or more." And the audience of Mary Noble in *Backstage Wife* endlessly heard the repeated plight of "the woman whose husband was the matinee idol of a million other women."

It would seem the Hummerts were writing for women whose relationships were on a slippery slope.

As an adult I heard that, supposedly, the Hummerts had a stockpile of labeled and cataloged plots that were recycled on all ten of their soaps with no concern about similarities. In those days a show required only two rehearsals and the fifteen minutes on air, with no memorization of scripts needed, so a good actor could play three separate shows a day. The Hummerts' reputation for recycling was further proven when an Iowa farm wife sent a letter to the lead actress in *Ma Perkins.* It said, "Dear Ma, I want you to watch out for that Pendleton guy. He's no good. He's out to trick you, because he's doing the same thing to Portia in *Portia Faces Life,* but he's using a different name."

Irna Phillips, on the other hand, did not recycle plotlines. When Irna graduated from the University of Indiana, she did not plan to be a writer. Instead, she wanted to be a drama teacher. But when she didn't get a job immediately, she joined a friend, Ireene Wicker, in a radio program entitled *The Singing Lady.* Ireene, who had a very nice voice, would sing, and together they recited poetry and sometimes told human-interest stories they had seen in the newspaper or heard about from neighbors. Irna and Ireene speculated on how the stories might conclude. Irna furnished the plots for these little tales, and the show became quite a hit.

One day, one of the sponsors said to Irna, "Miss Phillips, we wondered if you could make the stories a little longer, so they go on over several days." That meant each story would last fifteen minutes. Since Irna couldn't type, she enlisted her brother Arnold to type as she dictated. While Arnold typed, he kept his stopwatch beside him and would yell, "Stop! It's been fifteen minutes. It's time for the next episode." A young man at Procter & Gamble in Cincinnati heard about this program and told company executives. They contacted Irna, and the rest is history.

The more I thought about it, the clearer it became that my father was eager for me to receive the put-down that he fully expected Irna would give my work. As I sat on the lumbering bus that morning, I kept imagining the criticism Miss Phillips would have of *No Flags Flying,* the only script I deemed good enough to show her.

A small lady with piercing eyes, Miss Phillips invited me into her beautiful apartment on Lake Shore Drive. She introduced her secretary, and we all sat at a small table. Jumping right in, Irna asked me why I wanted to be a radio writer. Was it to make money? I told her that initially I wanted to be an actor but realized that a writer could play all the parts. She nodded and asked what my father's business was that he wanted me to go into. When I told her the company name— Perfection Burial Garment—she said, "Good God!"

Irna opened my script and started to read it aloud, page by page, right in front of me. I was stunned and embarrassed, wishing I could somehow escape. Her secretary put her hand over mine and said, "She does this all the time with new material." Here's how the script began:

THE NORTHWESTERN UNIVERSITY RADIO PLAY SHOP

TITLE: NO FLAGS FLYING

AUTHOR: Agnes Eckhardt, Spring 1944

ANNOUNCER: Ladies and gentlemen, this afternoon we are paying a visit to a home. An average-sized home in an average-sized town in the average-sized state of Iowa. We walk up the green lawn, pat the German police dog that lies on the porch, and enter the redbrick house. We go up the stairs to a small, den-like room, the walls adorned with many college letters and ribbons. To the left, Mr. O'Brien is seated before a large box he seems to be sorting. (VOICE FADES)

FATHER: Yes, I was just taking this Sunday off to go through a box of my son's souvenirs and sort 'em out. (SHORT LAUGH) When he left for the Air Corps he was so excited, he didn't put anything much in order. I remember he said though, "Don't throw any of those things away, Dad. They're all awfully important. Save 'em for me!" I guess you know how it is if you have a son. So I just thought I'd make this box look a little less like something the cat dragged in. You don't mind if I just go on while you're here, do you? You can pull up that footstool if you'd care to. It's over there, under that autographed picture of Frankie Parker.

(SOFT CHUCKLE) Now, who'd ever have thought Tim would be keeping this baby picture of himself? Think I'll just hang it up. It's painted on ivory in oils. I had it done as a surprise for Mother. Yeah, he was just five at the time. Certainly shows up that mass of black ringlets and blue eyes, doesn't it? He was an Irishman from the very beginning. Golly, I remember the day this was taken. Just after the three little fellows, Tim, the oldest mind you, had had an argument about an old swing I'd made for them from a discarded tire. (VOICE FADES)

VOICES: VOICES OF THREE CHILDREN ALL YELLING AT ONCE.

TIM: (ABOVE THE OTHERS) I wanna swing! I wanna! You let me!

BOB & ED: (FOUR AND THREE) No! No! No! Me! Me!

FATHER: (COMING ON MIKE): Here, here! What's all this trouble?

TIM: Daddy, make Ed and Bob let me swing. I wanta swing!

ED: I haven't had my turn!

BOB: Yes, you have, Ed. Yes you have!

ALL: (AGAIN GENERAL PANDEMONIUM) I wanna swing! Let me! Make him let me, Daddy!

FATHER (ABOVE THE DIN): Now just a minute! This is terrible! A disgrace! Don't you know you can't do this? You can't possibly cry in that swing!

ALL: (CRYING SUBSIDES TO FEW WHIMPERS)

*Later,*

TIM: Why?

BOB: Why, Daddy?

ED: Why?

FATHER: Good heavens! You mean you don't know?

ALL BOYS: (NOW REALLY CURIOUS) No!

FATHER: To think you've been swinging in this swing for almost two months; almost an age! And you never knew that this is a laughing swing!

TIM: A laughin' swing?

ED: Laughin' swing?

BOB: What's a laughin' swing?

FATHER: Yes, indeed, a laughing swing. And you only find them once every so often. No one can ever swing in that swing without laughing. (STARTS TO LAUGH) (FROM OFF MIKE A BIT) Look! I can't even go near it without laughing.

TIM: (CATCHING THE SPIRIT) A laughin' swing! A laughin' swing!

ED & BOB: (BOTH START TO LAUGH) Yeah, a laughin' swing! You go now, Timmy!

ALL BOYS: (LAUGHING TOGETHER)

SOUND: THE ROPE ATTACHED TO THE TIRE TWISTS AS THE TIRE SWINGS BACK AND FORTH ON THE LIMB. MIXED WITH CHILDREN'S LAUGHTER. FADES.

FATHER: (FADING IN) Guess you don't see laughing swings made out of tires these days, eh? Now what in time is this old chewing gum wrapper doing here? Certainly looks worn, doesn't it? (PAUSE) Say, you know what? This must be a souvenir from Tim's first airplane ride when he was ten. We were spending the summer at Lake Gogebic. It was . . . (FADES OUT)

SOUND: AIRPLANE MOTOR FADES IN SLIGHTLY.

FATHER: Tim persuaded his mother to take him up in one of those old-time aquaplanes that took ten-minute sightseeing tours. (VOICE FADES)

SOUND: BUILDS AND FADES QUICKLY. MOTOR UNDER ENTIRE SCENE.

MOTHER: Timothy, you must sit down!

TIM: Look, Mom! There's our cabins! See 'em!

MOTHER: Yes, dear, I see them.

TIM: (VERY EXCITED) Those sailboats look like my toy one, don't they! You see 'em, Mom? See 'em over there?

MOTHER: Oh, my, yes, Timothy! Please don't make Mother ask you to stay in your seat again, dear!

TIM: Golly gee! I wish I could fly. That's what I'll be some-day. You wait and see. Someday, I'll be a pilot. Only my ship'll be lots bigger and go lots higher and faster than this one! You wait and see! Golly gee! (VOICE FADES)

SOUND: AIRPLANE MOTOR UP AND FADE OUT

FATHER: (FADES IN) We didn't pay any attention to him then, but I guess Tim knew what he wanted, all right. Who'd have thought . . . Well, well! The rabbit's foot from the radiator cap of Tim's old model T2 we gave him for his sixteenth birthday. (FADES)

As Irna came to the end of the script—which follows Tim as he becomes an Army pilot who later dies in battle (and which can be found, in its entirety, at the end of this book)—I mentally prepared for the quickest way out. Instead, she closed the script, looked at me, and said, "How would you like to work for me?"

I could not believe my ears. Incredulous, I managed to ask, "Miss Phillips, are you serious?"

"Yes, very, and you are to call me Irna. Have you ever lis-tened to *Guiding Light*?"

"Yes, I love it!"

"You are going to dialogue its scripts from my outline. That's five scripts a week, for which I'll pay you one hundred dollars per week."

It was a fair wage for the work, but in the moment I was so thrilled that I hadn't even considered the money. "I can't think of anything I'd rather do than work with you."

After our meeting came to a close, I ran all the way to the bus stop. Hank and I had shared so much with each other, and at that moment I felt he was running with me.

"Did you hear what she said, Hank? I'm going to work for Irna Phillips!"

When I returned to my father's apartment, he was waiting for me, eager to gloat.

"Did you see that woman?" he asked.

"Yes," I said.

"So what did she say to you?"

I smiled. "She hired me."

"You're lying!"

I offered him her private telephone number if he wanted to check.

But all he said was, "You don't need me anymore."

Touched by this rare insight into his emotions, I put my arms around his shoulders and said, "But I do need you, Dad. I'll need you all my life."

He pulled away from me, grabbed his jacket, and headed toward the door.

"I have to get to the factory," he said, and left.

The next day, he said there was a nice studio apartment in the building, and that he would like me to move out of his place because it really wasn't convenient to have me there anymore. He added that he was sure I would be much happier by myself. And he was right, I was happier having my own place, but I still regretted our strained relationship—a situation I would always try to correct.

A short time later, my father ran into Irna and thanked her for helping his daughter.

Irna responded, "Mr. Eckhardt, I'm a businesswoman. I hired your daughter because she's good."

# Chapter 8

# FREEDOM OF OPPORTUNITY

Although my dream had come true by landing a job as a writer—for which I felt incredibly lucky—I could not get over missing Hank. Approximately six months passed before my best friends began saying I had to start living again. Even Hank's mother said that I must not think my life was over because Hank was gone.

But I couldn't simply alter my state of grief. On some deep level, I had not accepted Hank's death. So often, I awakened in the morning, happy because I had just dreamed that we were married. Then I would remember he was gone and deal with that reality all over again. I visited 1800 East River Drive often. It helped me to return to where Hank grew up with such a loving family, and his siblings did their best to cheer me up. His older brothers took me out in the evenings, and we would laugh so much. Because I had a job, they would say, "Come on, Ag, pony up. This evening is on you!"

There was much to-do about my having a job. Sometimes they visited Chicago and stayed in my small studio apartment in my father's building. They'd say, "Well, Ag, don't be a cheapskate. Where are you taking us to dinner?"

Of course, by kidding with me, they were trying to make me laugh. I really appreciated it and tried to appear like I was having fun. I always felt better with his family. But being with

Hank's brothers, as opposed to Hank, made me miss him even more.

The challenge of turning Irna's outlines into viable scripts helped to distract me from my mourning. Every morning at nine a.m. when I arrived at her apartment, Irna was ready to work. Since I knew Irna's long-term story outline by heart, I sat at the card table by the fireplace, ready to take notes. She told me how far I was to advance the story in that day's script. If we were trying to get ahead, we might do two or three ahead of time.

She might say, "You know when Bert Bauer is going to see her grandson in the hospital? You could have her encounter a friend who she had lost touch with. This would be a good opportunity to show Bert's warmth and humanity that the audience loves so much." Irna would often add something to the outline, such as, "When you do that friendship scene with Mike Bauer, let him say, 'Meta has adopted a child.'"

We ran through the notes session, which took about twenty minutes. If something came up that might affect the long-term plot, we could spend fifteen minutes to an hour exploring the possibilities. When Irna was finished with me, I headed back home with her instructions and sat at my typewriter, where I hoped I could lose myself in the Bauer family's town of Spring-field, Illinois.

I will never forget the evening when I finished a certain *Guiding Light* script. After stacking the script and carbon copy in my briefcase, I realized that those seven hours had been devoid of heartache for Hank. Gradually, I started to become social again, attending movies, visiting the art museum, and spending time with really good friends—when I wasn't busy writing, that is.

In college I had written many radio scripts—mostly about

teenage girls and inspired by the Priester house—that we produced and broadcast on the university's radio station. I was always proud to hear my scripts on the radio, and was especially thrilled that they were now airing on a commercial network. Meanwhile, television, an exciting and ambitious medium, was fast arriving on the entertainment horizon. But I had heard about so many attempts and failures that I opted to stick with radio, the most reliable opportunity at the time.

But that didn't mean that I stopped trying to grow as a writer. Radio writers had a union, the Writers Guild, that listed shows that accepted freelance submissions, including one called *Freedom of Opportunity*. Sponsored by Mutual of Omaha, it dramatized the lives of deserving Americans who made contributions to our country. I started listening to it every Friday evening at eight p.m. and found it to be an interesting and appealing series. Autobiographies and biographies were always my favorite reading—because truth is often stranger than fiction—and I was determined to have a script accepted by *Freedom of Opportunity*. I was also fortunate that Irna knew how much writing was helping me through a difficult time and approved of my moonlighting.

At the Chicago Public Library, I found a book of renowned American lives, and it became a gold mine for me. I chose to write about Dr. Howard Taylor Ricketts, whose claim to fame was discovering that the bite of an infected tick was the cause of Rocky Mountain spotted fever. As I crafted my episode on Dr. Ricketts's life, I paid attention to when the show's commercial breaks came and used those as a guide for the timing of each segment's dramatic climax. After quite a few drafts and a lot of hard work, I was finally ready to submit it.

.  .  .

THE FREEDOM SERIES was produced by the Arthur Meyer-hoff advertising agency in the Wrigley Building on Michigan Avenue. I'd never attempted to sell a script before, so I put mine in a manila envelope and took the bus to the Wrigley Building. The guild's list also stated that Nelson Shaun was the executive in charge of the program. In my naïveté, I said to the receptionist, "I'd like to see Mr. Nelson Shaun, please."

In a friendly way, she asked, "Whom shall I say is calling?"

I told her my name, and added that I had written a script for *Freedom of Opportunity.* As if this were a brand-new experience for her, she smiled and said, "Would you wait here, please?" She left her desk and returned to ask me to follow her to Mr. Shaun's office.

In his late forties, Nelson Shaun looked at me in a way that made me wonder if he thought I'd just graduated from kindergarten.

He motioned for me to sit down and said, "So you think you're a writer?"

I replied, "I know I am. I just want to be able to write more."

He asked, "Have you ever written anything?"

"Yes, I've written thirty-two and a half scripts for *The Guiding Light,* which were outlined by Irna Phillips. I work for her."

Irna's name got Mr. Shaun's attention, so I told him the whole story from the beginning, including my father's plans for my career.

"Burial garments?" he asked.

"For people to be buried in," I offered.

"Oh, I know what they use them for, but it's a business?"

"A very profitable one," I said.

"But you don't want to go into that line of business?"

"No. I would really like the opportunity to write for *Freedom.*"

In his sardonic voice Nelson said, "So you wrote a script? I hope it's good enough. Why do you want to write for *Freedom*?"

I said, "Because I love to do biographies."

He leafed through the pages of my script and said, "Has it got any schmaltz? You don't know what *schmaltz* means, do you?"

"No, I don't."

"You have to know the meaning very well if you hope to write for us. It means it's got guts, and it's what makes the listener like it and enjoy the show."

Suddenly, I realized he had just challenged me, and I wanted to take advantage of that.

"I think there is some schmaltz in my script, Mr. Shaun," I said.

He said, "Yeah? Where is it?"

"When Dr. Howard Taylor Ricketts looks down at the sick little girl with Rocky Mountain fever, and she looks up at him and says, 'Doctor, am I going to die?'

"'Not if I have anything to do with it,' Dr. Ricketts answers." I looked at him and asked, "Is that schmaltz, Mr. Shaun?"

He said, "I think it might grow up to be." He picked up my script. "Is your phone number on the script?"

"Yes," I replied.

He grabbed the manuscript out of my hands and said, "But I'm not Irna Phillips. I'm not going to make you watch me read it. I'll get to it on the subway going home. We'll be in touch."

The next day, Mr. Shaun's assistant put him on the telephone.

"We're going to give your script a chance, but you have to do a lot of rewriting. It needs a lot more schmaltz. Come in tomorrow at ten, and we'll talk about it."

*Schmaltz* was a word I had never heard before that day, but I would hear it many times in the future. He used it to describe all the changes he wanted in any given script, from cold-blooded murder, to death before dishonor, to love at first sight, to why the Seven Dwarfs fell in love with Snow White. And so, over a two-year period, I wrote about two scripts every four weeks for *Freedom of Opportunity*.

Writing for *Freedom* was very different from the work I'd done for *Guiding Light*. *Freedom* was a half-hour dramatization of a person's life, and it had to be engaging and suspenseful. I enjoyed both kinds of writing because they required such different approaches to the stories. I loved writing *Guiding Light* because it started my career, and I had so much admiration and respect for Irna's storytelling abilities. However, I found *Freedom* more interesting because I had to deal with the life of an actual person. One could say that my writing about real Americans would not take as much creativity as writing about fictional characters. But I relished the challenge of finding something that would make the stories of their lives resonate with an audience.

Among my biography subjects was chocolate company founder Milton Hershey (who sent me a gigantic box of his chocolates). In his case, I had to find a way to make an ordinary candy maker and his young wife exciting. They were striving to make a dream come true and finally it did. Catherine's love and patient encouragement brought them financial success, which they used to help their fellow man in their little town of Hershey, Pennsylvania.

In the case of Major Gregory Boyington, I had to find a way for the audience to connect to him. The famous World War II ace was called "Pappy" by his devoted squadron of twenty-seven misfits whom he molded into a remarkable fighting force.

Arriving on Guadalcanal, they discovered they had no planes or even a mechanic. Pappy and his pilots scrounged for damaged planes, repaired them, and took the fight right to the Japanese air bases. During eighty-four straight days of combat, Pappy had twenty-eight of their ninety-seven confirmed air-to-air kills. The Black Sheep Squadron fight over the Solomon Islands helped turn the tide of the war, and Boyington was awarded the Congressional Medal of Honor.

I wanted my listeners to understand the man behind the headlines, so my opening scene was Pappy rallying his squadron before the next dangerous mission. "Men, if you hear I've been shot down . . . don't you believe it. I'm just behind a cloud, ready to back you up."

My favorite of all was Martha Berry, a renowned Georgia educator. An affluent Southern lady, she summered in the Georgia mountains, and there discovered that Appalachian children had no structured education. Because my mother's job at the real estate agency did not provide a large income, we had spent many summers in the Smoky Mountains around Gatlinburg, Tennessee, and had been fortunate enough to meet a number of mountain people and learn about their way of life. Most of them were of Scottish descent, their forebears having come to the mountains to mine for gold. They stayed faithful to the homeland they would never see again, keeping traditions like making flowers from the hair of a horse's tail.

For dramatic reasons, I fashioned a fictional character named Ingaby Carpenter, who alerted Martha to the paucity of education for their children. The bond between my mother and me was closest at this time. She had met Hank when we visited Nashville at Christmas and was devastated at his loss because she'd loved him. My mother was so pleased when I sent her a copy of the script and wrote a note on the cover: "Dedicated to my mother, and our summers in the land of Ingaby Carpenter."

She wrote a very long letter to me—phone calls were too expensive—to say how much she loved Ingaby, how proud she was of me, and how much the dedication meant to her. It also made her very happy that I was launched in a career as a writer.

One of the nicest things about having Nelson Shaun as a boss was that I learned how to tell these stories in a way that he would like. Sometimes when he got an outside script submitted, he would ask me to rewrite it, adding, "What it needs is some of your schmaltz."

I quickly felt at home in Nelson's office. Among the "Freedies" who liked to hang out there and read each other's scripts was the gifted writer Studs Terkel. Many Chicagoans were fans of his Sunday night radio program, *Wax Museum*. Studs wrote almost as many *Freedom* scripts as I did. He and I were sitting in our special nook when Joe Ainley, the director of the series, entered with a script in his arm.

Highly frustrated, Joe said, "There's not an actress in Chicago who can get the mountaineer accent right!"

Studs took the script from Joe and opened it. He said, "Agnes, read the directions Ingaby gives to Martha."

I took the script, channeled the voices I remembered so distinctly from my summers in the Smokys, and read, "Atop b'ar mountain, down t'uther side a wee small bit. Jus' two small hoops and a holler from possum turn the brakes and the saddler creek. Hit's easy enuf ter find."

With a smile, Studs handed the script back and said, "Okay, Joe?"

Joe said to me, "Be at line rehearsal at seven."

When Nelson Shaun saw me, he said, "Five hundred actresses starving to death in the city of Chicago, and you write a part that only you can play!"

Studs started calling me "Ingaby" from that moment on, and soon everyone in the office called me that. As sorry as I was about the starving actresses, I did enjoy playing Ingaby. The whole cast was so helpful and forgiving when I goofed up a line. At one point, I said to Joe Ainley that I felt wearing shoes inhibited my portrayal of Ingaby.

"Kick them off!" he replied. So throughout the show, I stood at the mike barefoot. After the broadcast ended, the announcer told the audience that I needed to be barefoot to play the little mountaineer girl. He added, "By the way, she also wrote the script."

Whenever Nelson walked by the studio and saw me rehearsing, he would motion for me to leave the rehearsal and get to work on my scripts. Later, Nelson told me that he thought I did a pretty good job. He was a waspish man whose sometimes-sardonic humor offended others. But to me, he was one of the kindest people I had ever known.

AS MUCH AS I loved my job, my life wasn't all work in those days. My dear college friend Felicia Kerrigan had a brother named Jack who was a student at the Northwestern medical school in Chicago. One day, because he attended a surgical class at a hospital near my apartment, he offered to pick up Felicia—who was spending the night with me—and drive her to her place in the city. It so happened that Jack had five other medical students in his car, and they came up to my apartment with him "just to say hello."

I asked if anyone would like something to drink, and

everyone opted only for water. And then one of the friends, a man named Tom Bolton, suggested, "Let's order a pizza to go with the water." Later, while eating the pizza, Tom told me that he was in prep school at Lawrenceville and had always watched Hank at track meets. He then pointed to a young man named Tone Kelly, who had also admired Hank.

That coincidence turned us into a very friendly group, and lunch at my apartment became a tradition every Monday afternoon. As I found out later, Felicia and Jack had secretly plotted that introduction, aiming at helping me get on with my life. And indeed it was just that. No romance; just good friends enjoying spending time together. Those friendships lasted for a long time, and I will always be grateful to Felicia and Jack because they subtly introduced fun and friendship back into my life.

No matter how many emotions occupied my psyche, deep inside remained the desire to have a good relationship with my father. As I looked through my closet, to which nothing had been added since the fall before, an idea occurred to me. I called Harry, saying I needed to purchase a new suit, and since he had such great taste and knew what was right for me, I wanted his opinion on the outfits that I had previously tried on at Saks and Marshall Field's.

It was very pleasant going to the stores together. I bought the suit he recommended, and as we walked to Henrici's, he told me that a woman would be joining us. Her name was Hazel Schwab, and I liked her immediately. At dinner, Harry kidded her about growing up on a farm in Indiana. She said it didn't bother her to be kidded, and I could tell right away that she was very fond of him. She told me she worked in the watch department of Marshall Field's and had three sisters, all of whom were very close. I enjoyed talking to her, and when

Dad dropped her off at her apartment, I told her that I sincerely hoped to see her again. She said she hoped so, too.

I was surprised to see my father give her a rather quick kiss, but a kiss nonetheless. On the way home, Harry asked if I liked her, and I told him she was the nicest woman he'd ever introduced me to.

"Don't you like her?" I asked.

"Yes, but I'm not about to get married."

I wondered if Hazel might have other ideas.

As he left me at my apartment, he kissed my cheek good night. I felt that I was finally making some progress on improving our relationship. The next afternoon, deep in finishing a script, I heard his footsteps outside my studio and immediately recognized the angry tread. As I opened the door, he flung his finger accusingly at me and delivered his damning decree: "I know what you were doing last night, throwing in my face the fact that you can buy your own clothes!" Before I could defend myself, he turned quickly and disappeared into the elevator.

The fall of 1947 passed as I wrote *Guiding Light* scripts for Irna and an increasing number of *Freedom* scripts. The medical students had made a nice habit of having lunch at my apartment on Mondays, and whenever possible, weekends in Davenport helped me feel that life was worth living again. I went to Nashville and spent a peaceful Christmas with my mother and Aunt Emma, who by now were retired and living quietly together. Seeing that my mother's life had settled into a happy routine was a saving grace. She seemed to have overcome the pain that Harry had caused, and found satisfaction in her faith and her many church activities.

I also had wonderful visits with my beloved cousin David, who confided that he had found the girl he wanted to be his wife and the mother of his children. Although I was happy for him, I couldn't help wondering if I would ever realize the dream of having children of my own. Nevertheless, I reminded myself how fortunate I was to be a writer for a program that was both challenging and satisfying. In fact, I had just found a new American who could make a good story. I would be pitching the idea to Nelson Shaun as soon as I got back to Chicago.

On entering the Wrigley Building, I was anticipating my reunion with Studs Terkel, Joe Ainley, and Nelson Shaun. I took the hallway that led to Nelson's office, where we always gathered for our gabfest. I was about to enter when I heard Nelson's brother Myron's voice behind me. "Ingaby, don't go in." Myron Shaun was the account executive for Mutual of Omaha.

"Why not, Myron? Is the client in town?" I asked.

Myron's right hand held fast on the doorjamb. He said in a shaky voice, "Yesterday morning, Nelson had a massive heart attack. He's gone."

Sitting shivah at Nelson's home, I realized that I had cast him as a father figure. His kindness and his approval of my writing and my career in radio had been so encouraging. I also realized that I was now a grown woman who, as many of my friends said, needed a change in her life.

By the time I left the Shauns' I knew I wanted to leave Chicago and move to New York City to learn how to write for television. Like many other Americans, I was increasingly entranced by that new invention and its popular new shows: *Kraft Television Theatre*, *The Philco Television Playhouse*, *Westinghouse Studio One*—and New York was where such work was being produced. But if I did move, I couldn't work for Irna anymore.

I continued spending weekends in Davenport when I could, and surrounding myself with Hank's family and memories of where he grew up helped me contemplate my big decision. After giving the opportunity a great deal of thought, I realized that with Nelson Shaun gone, *Freedom of Opportunity* wasn't as enjoyable as before, and the idea of moving to New York became even more appealing. And when I asked Irna what she thought about it, she replied that if it was what I wanted, I should do it. I still missed Hank and considered Chicago home, so I was torn. But ultimately I decided I had to give it a shot.

In the winter of 1947, I was planning to go to Nashville and spend a peaceful Christmas there. The night before I left, Harry took me to dinner and gave me an enormous orchid corsage. But any hopes for a father-daughter rapprochement were eradicated with the first words he spoke when dinner was served.

"So you still think you can make enough money to support yourself with your ditsy writing-for-television idea?" he asked with a frown.

"I'm going to try," I said.

"Well, the doctor said my heart is still pretty good, so I'll give you two more years to fool yourself."

"What are you talking about?"

He went into yet another lecture about my taking over the business. Then he asked me to sign some papers, which his lawyer had said would make me a partner in Perfection. Harry claimed that the particulars of the partnership were too difficult for me to understand. Although my father would be the last person to sign anything without reading it, I knew that if I asked to read them, it would launch a tirade against my lack of trust. I cautiously complied, and then he closed the conversation by changing the subject.

After living in Chicago for many years, I finished packing for New York. I wondered if I should have insisted on Harry's explaining my involvement in his business. Perhaps signing those papers was a mistake—but it was too late now. I had other matters to attend to.

# Chapter 9

# NEW FRONTIERS

As I was leaving the *Freedom* office for the last time, I ran into Studs Terkel and we decided to have a farewell coffee. Toasting me with his cup, he said, "Mazel tov, Ingaby. To everything good in New York."

"Thanks, Studs. The truth is, I'm scared."

"Oh sure, that's because it's new. But you've got what it takes, Ingaby. It'll be a piece of cake for you. And didn't you say someone was writing a letter for you?"

"Yes, Virginia Payne." Payne was one of the best actresses in Chicago and, at age twenty-six, played the elderly character Ma Perkins. She was also very often in the cast on *Freedom of Opportunity.*

"Wow! She's a great actress," Studs said. "Who'd she write to?"

"To Max Wylie at the Young & Rubicam agency."

"I read his *Radio Writing* during my freshman year in college. He's a big wheel in New York. Max knows everybody in the business. He'll get you a great assignment."

"I just hope I can do a good job."

As he rose to leave, Studs added, "Don't sell yourself short, kid. And remember, piece of cake."

I packed my bags and took a taxi to the airport. The anxiety

I felt on the plane to New York was replaced, on arrival, by disappointment at the appearance of my new home. As the taxi pulled up to my new apartment on Manhattan's East Forty-Eighth Street, I was surprised that the entrance was two steps down from street level. It was what I learned was called a "basement apartment." I would also learn that it attracted a lot of street-level bugs. The front door opened and a woman identified herself as Mrs. Casey, the owner of the building. Without any words of welcome, she quickly gave me the history of the neighborhood, about which she seemed to have a very proprietary attitude. She missed "the old days" when it used to be full of friendly faces, and complained that it had filled with people who thought they were upper crust.

"Have you heard of Greta Garbo?" she asked.

"Of course. Does she live on this street?"

"More's the pity," said Mrs. Casey. "And also a couple named Dorothy Thompson and Sinclair Lewis. They're supposed to be married to each other, but I don't believe it."

The landlady showed me the minuscule apartment. The door in my bedroom led to a tiny backyard so dismal, I was shocked into silence.

Mrs. Casey added that the previous tenants had gone a step too far by having extravagant cocktail parties there. Betraying her Irish ancestry, she added, "Bad cess to the lot of them."

Then my apartment mate, Beth, arrived. The landlady left us, cautioning me to be thankful I had this place to stay because there was no room to be had on the island of Manhattan. Beth agreed with the landlady, adding other stories of homeless people. Clearly, she was intent on making me grateful to have this opportunity.

Beth added, "Before you unpack your things, I have to tell

you my one requirement of sharing this place with you. If you disagree, the deal is off." As she spoke, her eyes fixed on me intently.

"I'm in love with a married man and sometimes I need the apartment for us," she continued. "I will call you some evenings and tell you to go to a movie and see the feature twice, so we can have the place to ourselves. Then you need to call here to make sure it's okay to come back. I have to get back to the office now. You can give me your answer this evening, unless you have already left."

After she left, I walked out to our postage-stamp backyard. I sat down on the battered lawn swing, mulling over Beth's demand. As the sun hit my face, I realized it was the same sun that shone on Tennessee as well as in Chicago and Davenport, where I longed to be. But I knew that I had to give my writing career a chance.

Recalling Studs's comment, I said to myself, "Piece of cake, huh, Studs?"

The next day, I left fifteen minutes early so I wouldn't be late to the appointment Max Wylie's secretary had made with me. His large office proved that he was a big gun at the ad agency. Max showed me the letter he'd received from Virginia Payne, saying, "Ginny said you're top-drawer talent. She doesn't give compliments lightly. So you want to take a crack at television?"

"I do," I answered.

Max and I talked more about my recent arrival in New York, and then he said the words I'd been hoping to hear: "Agnes, you have a great résumé: *Freedom of Opportunity* and writing under Irna Phillips for *Guiding Light*. I'm planning on setting up an appointment for you with the producer for *Robert Montgomery Presents*."

I left his office, feeling like I might just be in the right place. When I got back to the apartment, my telephone was ringing. My father's secretary told me that he'd had a heart attack. My first thought was that he might have faked it to get me to agree to work with him at Perfection. Immediately feeling guilty for thinking that, and ever the dutiful child I'd been brought up to be, I prayed he wouldn't die, so that we would have time to build a normal relationship. I quickly made a reservation and left on the next plane to Chicago. During the flight I remembered that I'd had to postpone the meeting with Robert Montgomery and worried that it might jeopardize my work with the program.

Hazel met me at the airport and took me right to the hospital. She said he had looked so much better in the morning, but to me he looked ashen. When I arrived, he said, "What the hell are you doing here?"

Hazel spoke up. "Harry, she came to see you."

"Dad, is there anything I can do for you?" I asked.

"Yes, find me another doctor. This one says I have to quit smoking and stop playing the stock market."

When the doctor said we had to leave, Hazel and I had dinner in the hospital cafeteria. "I know he isn't always how you'd like him to be, but he really loves you," she said. And she so obviously loved him. The next day, I saw his doctor, who said he thought it was better if I went back to New York. "He thinks your being here means he is going to die, which is not a good thing for him."

"He's so terrified of dying," I said.

"Tell him good-bye in the morning, and that you're leaving because the doctor says he's going to be fine. I promise to keep you updated."

So I did just that, and left. A week later Harry went back to work at Perfection, but Hazel shared the welcome news that he had quit smoking. A few months later, she reported that they had purchased a beautiful vacation home on the Intracoastal Waterway in Palm Beach, Florida. It had a dock, and Harry had bought a sportfishing boat. I continued to send my letters, hoping to break through whatever demons possessed him. I had a feeling I was running out of time.

LIVING IN NEW YORK was both exciting and daunting. Many skilled broadcasting aspirants, including myself, clung to the dream that just being in the city would magically lead them to success and fortune. But the hard truth was that the only way to learn to write for television was by doing it. Luckily for me, my appointment with the producer had led to a writing assignment for *Robert Montgomery Presents*.

The show aired on NBC every Monday evening at eight p.m., and its hands-on writing process offered me the experience I so desperately wanted and needed. My first script, for which I was paid $750, was an adaptation of Mezz Mezzrow's autobiography, *Really the Blues,* and Jackie Cooper would star in it. I knew some male writers were paid more than me, but many of those writers were more seasoned and had a good track record. I had a rude awakening the next day when both the director and the producer grabbed me outside NBC's Studio 8H, waving my script in my face.

"Do you know what you have done? Written a script no one can produce!" they said.

The problem was that a commercial on an hour-long show was sixty seconds—hardly any time for an actor to change costumes, as my script required. I don't remember who had the bright idea, but at the line rehearsal we came up with the solution: Jackie Cooper, as Mezz Mezzrow, would wear an ample-sized raincoat under which he also wore a variety of shirts, one on top of the other, as he began his life story. When the narration ended, a bevy of hands tore the top raincoat off him backstage, and he began the next dramatic scene. And so it went, with Jackie, who appeared a bit heavier in the first scene, leaving a clump of discarded shirts that cluttered the floor.

For his performance, Jackie Cooper got a good review by Cyril Connolly of *Variety,* who also wrote, "Now I understand the purpose of television—well done." That review got me three future assignments for *Robert Montgomery Presents.* And so I learned from my mistakes, which is the only way to get good results. I was fortunate to get more writing assignments for *Hallmark Studio One, Philco, Goodyear Television Playhouse, Playhouse 90,* and *Armstrong Circle Theatre.* It was hard to believe, but my dream was coming true. I was a working writer.

During my first summer in New York, I went to visit Mother and Aunt Emma in Nashville. It brought me right back to my childhood: the summer breeze seemed to penetrate my skin, and the sky was a vibrant blue. Aunt Emma's ivy waved on the outside trellis, and I noticed that the back of a shipping crate still had my mother's handwritten numbers that recorded my childhood height. I realized the shipping crate had moved from the Russell Street house to Cedar Lane because it was a memento for them. I loved the cozy breakfast nook where Mother and Aunt Emma questioned me about what my life was really like in New York. And yet all I could think about was how much I loved being home, where I could eat my fill of turnip greens and beans cooked with ham hocks.

It was even nicer to enjoy my Southern specialties without the presence of my obnoxious roommate, Beth. It was a relief that I did not have to go to a movie so she could have her rendezvous with a married man. It was even nicer that I never had to meet him.

One day, the back doorbell rang, and an attractive young woman entered the kitchen. Her name was Jacqueline Hansard, and she was a French war bride whose husband had been an infantryman in her village in northwest France. She and my mother had met at church and developed a warm friendship. Jacqueline had made a coffee cake for us, but her big news was that she was pregnant and would soon go home to France to visit her parents while she could still travel.

I felt a tinge of envy, which happened every time I heard of a woman having a baby. This feeling was always accompanied by sad memories of Hank and the gnawing fear that I would be one of the many women who passed into her thirties and forties without having a child. Often I heard my father saying, "He's the only man who'll ever want to marry you."

My mother interrupted my worrying. "Aggie, Jacqueline is taking a ship to France that sails from New York." I knew that Mother understood my pain. She added, "Tell us more."

Jacqueline said she would fly to New York in a month, stay at a hotel overnight, and embark in the morning. When my mother looked at me, I knew what she was thinking, so I invited Jacqueline to spend the night at my apartment with me. Jacqueline was grateful, and I looked forward to trying to polish my French, which I'd studied in both high school and college.

When the week at home was up, I left feeling rested and tranquil. Mother and Aunt Emma were so happy in their little house that I had no worries about them. When I arrived in New York, I felt ready to start my assignment of adapting the *Robert Montgomery Presents* story "Little Boy Lost." It was about a boy lost in the war and adopted by the doctor who found him.

Soon after, Jacqueline arrived, and as I'd hoped, our conversations freshened my French. During her visit, she received a call from Étienne Villermont, a man whose home was near where her parents lived in France. He said he would come to see her off at the pier the next morning. She then started to describe him and laughingly said that in the French pecking order, he was considered a marquis, but nobody paid attention to that anymore.

Although Jacqueline had described Étienne, I was unprepared for the man I met. He was middle-aged and very good-looking. After we waved good-bye as the ship moved away from the pier, he invited me to have lunch with him. Thinking I could start writing the script later that evening, I accepted.

During lunch, Étienne filled me in on his family's fascinating history. After the French Revolution, many of the nobility had lost their money as well as their heads—his family included. As the eldest child, Étienne felt a responsibility to support his siblings. At Deauville, a wealthy American had befriended him and brought him into his mining business.

Étienne asked me if it sounded odd to feel that responsibility toward his siblings. I told him no, as I had the same feelings.

"You have siblings?" he asked.

"No," I responded. "It's about my mother. I'm an only child, and she's been divorced from my father since my birth."

"I look forward to meeting her someday."

"That's very kind of you."

Then Étienne changed the subject to my work.

"Jacqueline mentioned you're a writer for radio and television. Are you working on anything now?" I explained that I had put off "Little Boy Lost" to have lunch with him. And I had a future project adapting *Monsieur Vincent,* which would be an hour-long radio program.

"I'm really looking forward to it," I said. "I loved the movie, and it won best foreign film at the Oscars this year."

*"Oui bien!"* Étienne exclaimed. "I know the producer, Georges de la Grandière, and his wife, Monique. In fact, they're having dinner with me tomorrow night. You must join us."

I accepted, delighted to meet the producer of the screenplay I would be adapting for national broadcast.

After the taxi dropped me off at my apartment, I saw the waiting script of "Little Boy Lost." Putting that in the drawer, I pulled out the *Vincent* script and got ready to dive in so it would be finished before my dinner with the producer.

The next afternoon before dinner, I got a call from Étienne. He said, "I thought you'd like to know who will be at the dinner besides Georges and Monique. It will be the Honorable Hugh Gibson, who is the ambassador to Belgium, and his wife."

I thanked him, and as I hung up, I thought, *What a nice thing to do. He really is a thoughtful and impressive person.* The dinner was at the Metropolitan Club, which I knew by name only. It was outstanding and had a quiet elegance that registered with me as *le dernier mot.*

Some of the conversation that night revolved around the fact that I was adapting *Monsieur Vincent.* I told Georges that the hardest task was deciding which scenes to omit because of the limited airtime. Mrs. Gibson asked some very pertinent questions, quoting dialogue in French.

When I mentioned my admiration for Pierre Fresnay, the lead actor, they all agreed he was gifted, and Monique mentioned that she was especially close to his wife.

"She's a very dear friend of mine. Would you like to meet them both? They'll be in our Paris studio in a few weeks."

I said I would love to, but I could never afford a trip like that. Georges explained they were working on a short French history film called *Les Gisants*. "You could translate it if you'd like. It will be a business transaction."

Mrs. Gibson stepped in. "I see we are confusing you, Agnes. Please come to our apartment tomorrow at four p.m. for tea. I will help you straighten out the European trip we all hope you will make."

For some reason, they took me under their wing and announced how delighted they would be to see me in France in the summer. Ever since my French classes in college, I had yearned to go to the country. I began to count up my assignments to ensure I could cover the cost of my trip.

Life in New York suddenly became very pleasant, because Étienne was very attentive. He seemed to take for granted that we would see each other daily. Afternoon tea with the Gibsons also became a habit, and they began to treat me almost like their own child. Maybe it was because I was a girl and they only had a son, Michael.

Soon, I was helping Mrs. Gibson make and serve tea to her many distinguished friends and clean up afterward. At these teas, I had the privilege of meeting many fascinating individuals, including President Hoover, Mr. and Mrs. Theodore Roosevelt III, and many others in the upper echelons of government.

Étienne was very nice, very charming, and he made it clear that he intended to see me often over the summer.

At lunch one day, he talked about many places in France he would take me. I told him I couldn't afford the trip and could not accept his kind invitation. I was startled by his response.

"Agnes, I'm almost twenty years older than you. I've been waiting to find someone as delightful as you to do something like this with. Let me enjoy it! I have no expectations of you."

I decided to stop thinking about the imponderable and just enjoy the trip. As it turned out, the fee from my last three scripts and the translation work would pay for my transatlantic crossing.

A friend in the fashion business gave me a bon voyage gift that her company called "your weekend wardrobe." It consisted of a denim skirt, two T-shirts, and a scarf that one could tie nine different ways. The set retailed for the bargain-basement price of $9.95. It seemed like the perfect ensemble for a visit to a country home.

I took a boat over to France because Étienne told me I would enjoy the experience. For extra spending money, I accepted a writing job from General Mills to solicit testimonials for their products for advertising copy. My particular charge was Betty Crocker's instant soup, of which the ship's chef gave a glowing review.

Étienne greeted me at Le Havre, as he had flown home a week earlier. We met Monique and Georges, who had invited me to spend the weekend at their summer place on the Loire River. Quickly I accepted, thinking this would be the perfect place for my weekend wardrobe. Étienne and I were in the backseat as Georges explained that we were driving through the Loire Valley. As the car went through a pair of majestic columns, I thought we were entering a lovely park. After some time, a breathtaking castle appeared on the horizon and Monique said, "*Voilà, chez nous.* We are here."

Speechless, I thought to myself, *Girl, you're in big, big trouble.* Monique and Georges sensed my discomfort and tried very hard to ease it. Yet it was hard to overlook the regal seven-hundred-year-old structure, and the fact that they had their own vineyards, from which we were served champagne *nature* at various times in the six salons on the first floor. Monique explained that their forebears had the château built with many parlors so that any time during the day, there was always a room with sunlight.

At dinner, since I was the guest of honor, at my place was a sterling silver frame with a dinner menu written in purple ink. Sitting next to me was their youngest daughter, Armelle, whom I tried to engage in conversation, but she only stared at me, making me wonder how bad my French was. Soon her mother came to my rescue, touched my hand, and said, "*Ma cherie,* I forgot to tell you. We do not permit our children to speak during dinner until dessert."

From the castle, Étienne drove me to join Jacqueline at her parents' house. On the way, I noticed the Normandy apple orchards had been decimated. "The Nazis destroyed whatever they could as they retreated," Étienne explained.

Jacqueline's parents did all they could to make me feel at home. When I said I would like to press a dress, an ironing board and iron were produced very quickly. To my shock, the iron had been heated on the gas stove and gave me quite a burn. Madame Jourdrier was very apologetic for failing to tell me that the iron did not have an electric cord, which I had missed completely.

Étienne had invited Jacqueline and me to a welcome dinner at the Casino Barrière de Deauville. During dinner, Étienne gave a bit of history of the famous casino, where confirmed gamblers could lose up to ten thousand francs a night with aplomb.

I had also told Étienne I wanted to visit Omaha Beach. The next morning, I stood on one of the high bluffs overlooking the English Channel. The contrast between the opulence of the gaming room and the bleak expanse of sand couldn't have been more glaring. D–Day had only been six years earlier, and the newsreels of the invasion ran through my mind. There was General Eisenhower giving his simple last command to the young men he had chosen to hit the beach at dawn. "Good luck! And let us all beseech the blessing of almighty God upon this great and noble undertaking." Then soldiers jumped from the landing craft into the surf and ran straight toward the withering German machine-gun fire, exhibiting selfless courage. I thought of all the women who were waiting for their loved ones and how they must have felt. I realized they were suffering deeply, too—that I was not alone. I was trying to tell myself I was very lucky to be where I was and with the friends I had. Looking into the clouds, I remembered the lines of the farewell card written by Hank's cousin Lieutenant Walter J. Walsh after he heard that Hank was MIA. Hank's parents had it printed for his memorial service.

To Hank . . .

We looked ahead that night to meeting soon again. Ignored time fleeting. Casualties and squadron losses . . . But fighter planes resemble crosses. As they lean against the sky. And on a cross men sometimes die. I think a cross must be the altar of sacrifice—when humans falter. L'envoi.

So long, Hank, old boy. God bless you. Pray for us that in distress we too can earn your epitaph. "Living with Death, he kept his laugh."

Looking at the beach, I realized that Hank was really gone.

# Chapter 10

# SEARCH FOR TOMORROW

Walking back to the car, Étienne wondered if seeing Omaha Beach was too much for me. I shook my head and said, "No, I needed to come." It was a beautiful area; the temperature was balmy, and the jasmine was abundant.

"Do you think you would like to live here?" he asked.

"What are you talking about?" I responded. "I have a writing job in New York."

Étienne took my hand and said, "*Ma petite* Agnes. You have to know that I love you. I want to spend the rest of my life with you. I know it comes as a surprise, but I would like you to think about being married to me. I think you will find you will be very happy with me. I won't press you, but will you tell me you will think about it?"

I realized Étienne was right; I wasn't totally surprised at his declaration, although the thought of marrying him was new to me. I was very fond of him, but I hadn't considered the prospect. Still, Hank had been gone for over six years, and I knew I wanted to be married and have a family, so I said, "Yes, I'll think about it."

He nodded in a way that indicated he realized I was torn. "I also know you were very much in love with someone who is gone. I understand that very well, but I believe I can give you a very good life. Now, let's get back to Paris for our dinner."

On the return drive to Paris, I thought to myself, *I love him, but I'm not in love with him. Perhaps that's not a necessity for a good marriage. I have had one great love, but he is gone. Étienne is a lot older than I am, but I believe I could make a good life with him and be a good wife. I want to have children, and I do think he would be a wonderful father.*

Étienne had planned to take the return flight with me to New York, but a doctor had said his mother needed a series of tests, so he stayed with her in Paris. On the plane, all I could think of was Étienne's proposal. There were so many good things about him. I was leaning toward saying yes, but I remained undecided.

The plane landed in New York and I was back to reality. I called my father's secretary, and she reported that the doctors were pleased with his recovery. She also gave me the surprising news that he had married Hazel. Hazel's sister Elsie had been insisting that Hazel was too easy on Harry, and she implied to him that if he didn't marry her sister, he was going to lose the best nurse he'd ever had. I was overjoyed with the news and sent a letter full of good wishes for both of them. Hazel called me to thank me for the letter and said she was going to do everything she could to make him change his attitude.

In New York, tragedy struck when Mrs. Gibson, whom I had so enjoyed helping with her afternoon teas, suffered an unexpected heart attack and died. After her death, I truly became a member of the family. Because the ambassador received so many letters and messages of condolence, I was appointed to respond to each with a personal thank-you. One particularly memorable one was signed "Elizabeth Regina"—the queen of England. I was glad to help Mr. Gibson in my spare time, even though my writing assignments were demanding.

Although very grateful that my shows aired at night, I still wanted to write a daytime serial. I was particularly interested in introducing social relevance to daytime by tackling the problems that humanity saw and faced. While I waited for the right opportunity, I stayed in touch with Irna, although it had been three years since I had written dialogue for *Guiding Light*. But soon after my return from France, I was surprised when I answered the telephone and it was the show's producer, Roy Winsor.

Roy announced that he had moved to New York City to head the television department of the Biow Company, an agency that handled several of Procter & Gamble's accounts. Then he invited me to lunch, to "talk business." At lunch, to my surprise, a Biow lawyer accompanied Roy, who asked if I would like to write the first soap opera for television—the ideal program I had thought about for so long. He told me I was very good at the "nuts and bolts" of a soap opera and had a terrific ear for dialogue. He said he'd enjoyed listening to my *Guiding Light* scripts for Irna. "They were tops," he added.

To say that I happily agreed is an understatement. I was thrilled as Roy described what a wonderful and gratifying future I would have. He said, "Don't worry about the scripts for your creation; let's get to the story and characters. We have plenty of time for that."

He nodded to the lawyer, who handed me a contract. It read, "I, Agnes Eckhardt, agree to furnish plotlines and characters for a new televised daytime serial. The compensation will be discussed at a future date." The whole thing seemed such a wonderful opportunity that I didn't even stop to think when that future date might be. I eagerly signed the no-fee contract, which the lawyer put in his briefcase. I felt sure that a wonderful career was about to unfold.

Roy said, "My secretary will set up an appointment with

Procter & Gamble, which will be on our team. That's when you will tell us what the show will be about and how it will be a winner. So get to work, girl!"

I wound up writing a long-term story of a young wife, Joanne Barron, whose husband was being overridden by his father. She would have to fight her father-in-law for her husband's independence, the survival of their marriage, and the well-being of their children. As I arrived at my apartment, thinking of calling my mother to tell her about the big opportunity, the telephone was already ringing. It was my father.

There was no greeting, just the question, "Did you get my letter?" When I said no and asked what the letter was about, he said, "All you need to know is that I meant what I said to you, and I don't think you can change my mind. Do you understand?" I told him I did and before I could say anything else, he hung up and I was holding a dead line.

Thoughts of being the head writer of the first television soap opera overtook the disconcerting possibilities of my father's call. Finally, after deciding what subject would resonate with the soap opera audience, I fell into a peaceful sleep.

Alas, thinking that my father's letter would have no severe consequences was a huge mistake. In the morning, I was awakened by the doorbell and a special delivery from my father. His letter began by saying, "After much thought to the cavalier belief that your mother has instilled that you can make your way as a writer, I have come to a decision for my own peace of mind, as well as my good health. I'm putting the choice to you that if you don't follow my wishes and come to Chicago and work for me, you will be immediately disinherited. If you fail to answer my letter, your inheritance will be struck from my will."

I had just been offered this amazing job. It seemed

impossible to let my father destroy that opportunity. The agony of this Hobson's choice plagued me all morning until Mr. Gibson's secretary called to remind me of my lunch with him. I assured her I would be there.

My self-confidence was so shattered, and I was so demoralized by my father's insistence that I had no talent, that while getting dressed, I began thinking about giving up writing. I decided I would ask Mr. Gibson if he thought I was qualified to be a secretary to one of his many distinguished friends.

As we waited for our meal, I gathered the courage. "Do you have any friends that could use me as a secretary? I'm a fast typist, and my mother had me learn shorthand in high school."

Mr. Gibson said, "Surely you're not thinking of giving up your writing? You've been doing so well."

I handed him Harry's letter. "If I could get a regular job, I could try to write in my free time," I said.

"This is outrageous," Mr. Gibson said.

"That's my father. He has always said I have no writing talent. Now his letter says he will disown me unless I move back to Chicago and run his burial garment business."

"Is there a large inheritance?"

"I don't know and don't really care. He paid for me to go to college, but I have been supporting myself as a writer since graduation. He already gave me one-third of Perfection, but I don't receive any revenue from that."

"I know someone who might be able to help. He's the smartest man I've ever worked with."

He jotted a number and address on a notepad. I felt terribly embarrassed and started to apologize. "I shouldn't have bothered you with this. I'm so sorry."

"Don't be sorry. Just be honest with him, and tell him everything you told me. Show him this preposterous letter from your father and don't worry about anything. The fee will be waived."

When I realized what he was doing for me, the tears started again.

"How can I ever thank you?"

With a gentle smile, he said, "My dear, I feel I'm still in debt to you for all the help you gave Mrs. Gibson in serving our friends their afternoon tea." Then he handed me one of the menus and said, "Now, let's decide with what outrageous dessert we're going to indulge ourselves."

A WEEK LATER, I sat in the most beautiful office I'd ever seen and listened to Mr. Gibson's lawyer take great pains to explain the contents of the letter he had drafted.

"The key," he stressed, "is that you say in your letter that you will gladly return to Chicago to work, if—and only if— you are permitted to buy the business from him. The letter also must detail why it makes financial sense for you both." The lawyer added, "Which it does, I assure you, because you'll pay for it with your profits."

He explained I had to rewrite it in my own vernacular, as if buying the business were my idea. The following are a few excerpts.

April 12, 1950

Dearest Dad:

Let me begin this letter by telling you that I do most fully appreciate the fact that in this matter of the business you are thinking only of my welfare, and I am deeply grateful. During all the hours and days of my thinking, the two aspects which I have placed in prime importance are, first, that you most certainly have every right to enjoy, in terms of relaxation, leisure, and the Florida climate, a respite from the business to which you gave so many years and which made such a success; and secondly, as you told me, that I would be shortsighted not to realize the worth of the business and wish it to continue.

I have decided, Dad, that I would be willing to take over the business, but I do not think it would be fair to me to take over the business without my actually owning it. As the situation now stands, I own one-third of the business and the balance, of course, I would have to pay you for.

The reason for my wanting to buy your interest is that in selling your two-thirds to me, you would only have to pay tax on long-term capital gains which, at the very most, would amount to only 25 percent of the total amount of the sale. However, in the event of your death, the inheritance tax would be much greater than this. Now, we both know that, fortunately, your health is very good. Dr. Amptman has assured both of us of this, and I am happily confident that you have many years of life to enjoy. But this, businesswise, makes it all the more practical from my standpoint that I would not care to spend many years running the business and then have to face an exorbitant estate tax on your two-thirds when it could be avoided.

Dad, I think you must realize by now that I have never attempted nor harbored the wish to have any of your money. As I told you over the phone, what you do with it is strictly your affair, as I have not done anything to merit it. And believe me, the most important thing to me is that you have a long and happy life as free of worry and cares as possible. And I think your plan of living in Florida would be wonderful for you. But when we discuss a serious business matter such as this, with all its ramifications, then it is only good business to insist on this procedure. If I did not insist upon it, I would not be showing the business acumen and competence necessary to carry on the business.

Lots of love,
Agnes

Dad's secretary, a friend of mine, later reported to me that my father and his lawyer, Bob, were in his office when they received my letter. Bob slit open the envelope and handed it to Harry, who was jubilant with anticipated victory. Because he wanted to study the faces of those present, he said, "You read it, Bob." As Bob read from the letter, "I would be willing to take over the business, but I do not think it would be fair to me to take over the business without my actually owning it," my father became apoplectic. He said, "What the hell is she talking about?"

Bob said, "She explains what she means, Harry. Listen."

As he finished reading my letter, Harry started screaming while pounding the desk. "Where did she ever get such an idea? It's impossible."

To which Bob replied, "Harry, she's right."

My father never spoke to me about his business or my writing again.

# Chapter 11

# BEST MAN

By 1950, I was finally getting enough work to afford to live alone. After several searches, I found a lovely one-bedroom apartment at 405 East Fifty-Fourth Street. I was happy to say good-bye to my roommate, Beth, and her constant proclamations that her married lover was going to divorce his wife and marry her. I was enjoying putting my things away when the telephone rang.

An unfamiliar man's voice said, "Agnes, this is Bob Nixon."

My mind flashed back to the med students who came to my apartment every Monday for lunch. One of them, who was named Bob Nixon, had quite a unique voice. It was so deep, his friends used to refer to him as "Sexy Voice." The voice on the end of the line was quite different, but I blamed it on a bad connection. I asked, "Are you in New York?"

He replied, "No. I'm in Washington, but I would come to New York if we could arrange a date to meet."

"That would be lovely," I said, wondering why he was in DC.

"If you could hold on, I'll get my date book."

I asked, "Have you seen any of the other guys?"

"Lots of them. I'll tell you about them when I see you."

By now, I couldn't blame the caller's voice on the bad

connection. This person had a crisp Midwestern accent. I said, "Bob, you don't sound like yourself."

To my surprise, he replied, "How would you know? You've never talked to me before."

I exclaimed, "Oh! You're *that* Bob Nixon!"

Obviously not pleased with being categorized as "that," he replied, "Yeah, I'm 'that' Bob Nixon. I only called you because Katie Priester made me promise that the next time I was back East, I would meet you."

Suddenly, it became clear what Hank's mother was trying to do. She had mentioned a young man who worked for the Chrysler Corporation and who was the same age as Hank would have been. I also remembered that Eda, now a freshman in college, had mentioned having a monumental crush on this Bob Nixon, although he had never asked her out on a date. When Katie had come to New York, she had spoken glowingly of Bob, but had added that she didn't think anything would come of Eda's interest in him because of their ten-year age difference. The question remained: Why would Katie want me to meet a man her daughter was so taken with?

As Étienne was not coming to New York for two weeks, I told Bob that next weekend was fairly free. We decided that he would come to New York in time for dinner Friday evening. Then he added, "And on Saturday I'll need your help in buying a Christmas present for Eda."

Well, that made the mystery deepen. If he was buying a gift for Eda, she must have gotten his attention, but if that were the case, how would she feel about my meeting him?

I spent the rest of the week finishing a script for *Hallmark Hall of Fame,* which, incidentally, was a televised version of the biography of Martha Berry that I had written for *Freedom of*

*Opportunity* some years ago. I let the *Hallmark* producer listen to my transcription of that show and he told me to go ahead, saying he thought we could make a good show. In my spare time, when I thought of spending much of my weekend with Bob Nixon, I feared it would be tedious.

In fact, it was just the opposite. When I opened the door, I thought, *Eda is right. He is good-looking.*

Bob said, "You don't look like your picture."

"You mean the one at the Priesters'?"

He nodded.

"Why not?" I asked.

He said, "I thought you looked like the coldest fish I've ever seen. But Katie insisted I come and meet you."

He came in for a drink, and later, over dinner, we talked about all the friends we had in common in Davenport and updated each other on events in their lives. With so much history in common, we quickly fell into a comfortable friendship. Katie had told Bob about my writing, which he said he found impressive, and I got caught up in his enthusiasm for the car business. According to him, it would help rebuild America after the war.

When I told him how Hank and his brothers kept a competitive Ping-Pong ladder, Bob said, "I sure know why you loved being part of the family. They made me feel the same way."

Bob surprised me by adding, "Katie told me how much you and Hank meant to each other. Do you want to talk about him?"

I said, "Hank's mother has probably covered that well."

Bob said, "I hope you don't mind my mentioning Hank. I, too, thought I would have been married many years ago, but I ended up with a broken heart."

When he told me that he had drawn Eda's name from her family's gift pool, I wondered if what I felt was relief. On Saturday we went to Bloomingdale's to select a present for her. We were on the escalator with lots of children, and Bob began to talk to them.

"Hey, are you going to see Santa Claus?" he asked. "What are you going to ask him for? Oh, that's good. I'll bet he'll bring you that."

Suddenly there was a warm spot inside me that I hadn't felt for quite a while. That day, Saturday, December 10, 1950, was also my twenty-eighth birthday, and a friend of mine invited us to her apartment for cocktails. After that, Bob and I had dinner at a lovely French café.

He asked, "Is this your twenty-eighth birthday?"

"Yes."

"Don't you want to get married and have children?"

"What are you talking about?" I demanded. "I'm not getting old."

To which he observed, "Well, you're not getting any younger."

"Are you always so honest?"

"I try to be. Some people don't like it. Does it bother you?"

I said only, "Not really." Yet I admitted to myself that I found his honesty rather appealing.

The next morning, we went to church together, and after mass we stopped at a bakery for a special pastry to take back to the apartment to have with coffee. On entering the building, the doorman said quietly to me that I had received flowers. He had a key to my apartment and had kindly put them on the table for me. I knew they had been sent by Étienne, who was in Paris on business. Two dozen beautiful, long-stemmed red roses decorated the apartment. I felt a little guilty about Etienne because during the evening I had not given him a moment's thought.

Seeing them, Bob said, "Oh, I see my flowers came."

"You didn't send those flowers," I said.

To which he replied, without missing a beat, "Don't tell me that they put the wrong name on the card!"

I topped him with, "Where's your honesty now?"

He laughed and said, "One for you!"

Then he proceeded to take out a box of birthday candles from his pocket and put them into the sweet rolls.

He said, "Happy birthday. You don't look twenty-eight."

I laughed and thanked him. Then he took out his Amtrak train schedule. "This is for next weekend."

"Are you coming back?"

"No. You're coming to Washington."

"No, I'm not," I said emphatically, thinking it was too soon.

"When was the last time you visited the capital of your nation?"

I had to confess, it was when I was at Catholic University on scholarship, eight years ago.

Then he said, "You should be ashamed of yourself. The train ride is pleasant, but the flight is so much faster, and then you can get there in time for us to go to dinner—"

I broke in. "I haven't said I'm going."

"But you have to. You'll get to meet the guy who shares my apartment, and also, you'll see Maury Donnegan. You know Maury from Davenport, don't you?"

"No, I don't know Maury."

"This will be a perfect opportunity to meet good ol' Maury. He's a great guy."

"I'm not particularly dying to meet Maury Donnegan."

"But you said you haven't been to Washington in a long time. Isn't that a good enough reason to come? By the way, thanks so much for helping me select Eda's present."

"I think she'll like it. The colors are right for her."

"She will like it because you helped me pick it out."

"Are you going to tell her that?" I asked.

"Why wouldn't I?"

"Her mother told me she was pretty gaga over you. Maybe still is."

"Would you care?"

"You'd better hurry. You may miss your train."

"Right. I'll call you tomorrow night."

With that, he put his arms around me and gave me a real kiss. And I liked it. He just looked at me and kissed me once more, and then he was gone. As I walked into the living room and looked at Étienne's red roses, I knew I'd be taking the five o'clock plane to our nation's capital.

THE NEXT WEEKEND, Bob was waiting at the gate when my plane landed, and he kissed me hello when we met. It was great to see him. After we got in the car, he kissed me again and handed me a hatbox.

"This is for you," he said.

"What is it?" I asked.

"A hat."

"But I don't need a hat," I said.

"But I need you to take it."

"Why?" I asked.

"Because you said last week that if a man bought you a hat, you would marry him."

"I did not say any such thing," I protested.

"Why do you think you didn't say it?"

"Because it's such lousy dialogue."

"Put it on. I want to see how it looks," Bob insisted.

"Wait 'til I get to the ladies' room of the restaurant."

In that mirror, with the hat on, I looked like a Spanish matador, which is exactly what I told Bob.

"The prettiest matador I've ever seen," he replied. "How's that for dialogue?"

"Not bad."

Bob said, "So you've turned in five scripts for your show this week?"

I nodded. "The first five episodes are when the show begins, so that's why we're meeting with the Biow advertising agency on Monday—for notes. They produce the show for Procter & Gamble."

As we ate, Bob asked me more about my work. "Notes? What are they?"

I explained that notes were comments on story points that would be developed later after the first five scripts had aired. I told Bob how I was really looking forward to that meeting because I felt I did a good job in the scripts of setting up the problems that Joanne Barron, the lead character, had to face.

"What is the main problem?" Bob asked.

"Joanne is very much in love with her husband, but her father-in-law is determined that his son will follow him in his business. It has a familiar ring, doesn't it?" I had told him about my father.

Bob said, "Yes it does. Would you let me read your scripts?"

"Do you really want to?"

"I want to know everything about you. Particularly the

things that mean the most to you. I bet I'll learn some of that from your writing."

While eating dinner and looking at this man, I felt my heart beginning to open to him. I felt like I knew him; there were so many things about us that just seemed to fit. He loved children and said he would like to have them. He was a practical person. He asked me so much about Hank, and he obviously understood how much I had loved him. He talked about Hank's parents and how they had made Hank the kind of person he was. In every way, we seemed to have a lot in common. I wore my matador hat for the rest of the weekend. The next week I told Étienne about Bob. He was resigned to the fact that I had fallen in love with someone else, and his reaction was in keeping with the gentleman he had always been.

On Monday morning, when I entered the Biow conference room, I was surprised that the client wasn't there, and also by Roy's announcement that he had brought a man named Charlie Irving onto the team. Roy said that Charlie was a longtime friend who had worked on previous soaps as a director and producer. Roy announced that Charlie was going to be a producer on *Search for Tomorrow* and how terrific he was. He also told me that Charlie would be my new boss. It all felt wrong, and I immediately felt uneasy about the future.

Charlie Irving's first words were, "Well, let's get to it. We have rather big trouble here, Agnes."

"What kind of trouble?"

"Well, actually, the basic thrust of your story."

"My story? Everyone approved it."

Roy said, "Charlie has given us a new perspective on it."

Bewildered, I asked, "You don't like the story projection I outlined?"

Before Roy answered, Charlie cut in, "We're not going to get an audience with all that psychodrama."

"It's not psychodrama," I said.

"Of course it is. You're making everybody feel they should take their problems to a shrink."

I turned to Roy. "The client approved these stories. So did you."

"Charlie has made us see it in a different light," he repeated.

"And the client agreed with him?"

Charlie was firm. "Listen, Agnes. I know this is a shock to you. Maybe you can try to rewrite these scenes, if you like. And we can help you."

"Who is saying what the basic story should be?"

"I was hired to do that," Charlie said.

Trying to soften things, Roy cut in, "Don't get so upset, kid. You're an important writer on our team."

"I thought I was the head writer."

"Oh, sure. That's the title you have, but listen, let's stop all this wrangling and see if we can't put some real passion and—"

Charlie cut in, "And some real basic sex! We've got a lot riding on this. So let's start with episode one."

With a sick feeling in the pit of my stomach, I took out my script for the first episode, which would have no relevance to what they obviously were looking for. I tried for days to write the kind of scripts Charlie Irving wanted, but by the end of the week, I became convinced that what he wanted was me off the show. When Bob flew in on Friday, it felt so good to be able to tell him what had happened.

"Honey, you've got to leave that damn show."

"I can't."

"Why not? Do they still owe you a lot of money?"

I nodded my head.

Bob said, "How much do they owe you?"

"I don't know."

"Don't know? In your contract, how much does it stipulate they'd pay you?"

"I never got any specific amount. I wrote all those treatments and just put them in the mail. They just said they were excellent shows and that they had sent them on to their producers."

"You mean you started all this work without settling your pay?"

"I'm afraid so."

"Honey, that's terrible."

At that very moment a certified letter arrived at the door. It was from Biow and P & G, and it stated that I was being removed from the show.

Bob was outraged. "Honey, you've been shafted."

"I guess this is what that boss had in mind when he said I'd never be a writer. Now what do I do?"

Bob put his arms around me. "Marry me and have a baby."

"Do you think I'd marry you just because I was fired?"

"I would hope you'd marry me because you love me."

"And you know I do," I said.

Bob put his hand on my shoulder and faced me with a stern look. "I need serious verbal confirmation on this," he said. "Will you marry me?" I threw my arms around him, saying, "I thought you'd never ask." Laughter gave way to a passionate kiss.

As my hand touched Bob's face, I felt a tremendous emotional and physical attraction to this man. I knew I would say yes. "Bob, first I have to tell you something—"

"I don't mean to interrupt, but I know you're going to tell

me you're a writer. That's one of the things that makes you you, and it's why I love you. And it's why I want us to get married and spend our lives together."

"This is what I didn't want you to interrupt." I gave him another big kiss, and we were engaged.

# Chapter 12

# SETTLING DOWN

My wedding day was April 6, 1951. At twenty-eight, I was a very happy woman because I would soon marry the handsome twenty-nine-year-old Bob Nixon, who was charming, funny, and just irresistible. We found that we thought alike and were very happy together.

I was calm because my inner sense told me that with this man, I could make the family I had always dreamed of. Mother and Aunt Emma came up from Nashville a few days early to get to know Bob; I had told them all about him. They liked each other immediately, and we had fun visits together.

My father had said he would not contribute a cent to the wedding. Instead of fighting, I told him it would mean a great deal if he would give me away, and he agreed to do so. There was only one unpleasant situation. Bob had to get a marriage license in New York at nine a.m. the morning of the wedding, but my father's train arrived at the same time. He expected me and Bob to meet him on the platform, and he took it as a personal affront when neither of us was there. When we went to Dad's hotel room later that day, Bob was so ingratiating that a crisis was averted.

We didn't have a rehearsal dinner, but my friend Doris Weston held a small gathering with a buffet supper. I was very worried that my father would make a scene when he saw my mother, but she drew upon all her Southern charm. When she saw him, she smiled and said, "Good evening, Mr. Eckhardt." Contrary to my fears, the night was very pleasant.

Our wedding was a simple but lovely affair in the chapel at St. Patrick's Cathedral. Hank's parents were very happy about our marriage, and it was wonderful to have them there. Unfortunately, my cousin David, who was like a brother to me, could not come to the reception. It was held at Sherry's restaurant, where we had a luncheon and music for dancing.

Afterward, we drove straight to our new apartment in Philadelphia, where Bob had been recently promoted to manager of Chrysler's mid-Atlantic headquarters. Thankfully, our new home was convenient for my job, too. I could write anywhere, and whenever I needed to have a face-to-face meeting, New York was only a two-hour train ride away.

The next morning the milkman made a delivery and said, "Thank you, Mrs. Nixon."

We were such newlyweds that Bob asked, "What name did he call you?"

"Mrs. Nixon—and I like it."

As I adjusted to married life, my mind went back to writing, as it always did. Bob's support helped me survive the blow of being fired from *Search for Tomorrow*. He said, "Listen, I'm your corner man. Of course you're depressed; a sucker punch knocked you down. But, honey, you're a winner, so you've got to pick yourself up and get back in there and fight. Show them that 'woman writer' doesn't mean inferior." Giving him a hug, I said, "This woman writer sure feels a lot less inferior with you in her corner."


BECAUSE BOB HAD just been promoted, we had to wait for a proper honeymoon. Instead, that fall, we decided to go see my family in Nashville, my father in Chicago, and the Priesters in Davenport.

Nashville was certainly pleasant. Mother and Aunt Emma held a reception for us at their house and invited the many friends who had known me since I was a little girl. It was very nice, and Bob, of course, was a big hit. Among the guests was my cousin Birdy Ryan, a brilliant woman who, decades later at ninety-five, would still be the top librarian at the Nashville Law Library. I was very fond of Birdy and enjoyed her keen mind but was always dismayed by her racial views. After some pleasant conservation, she asked if we knew that they were trying to let colored people into the schools.

"It's just terrible, Agnes. I was hoping you would come and fight with us."

Gripping Bob's hand, I said, "Birdy, I'm *for* integration."

Her jaw literally dropped. "My God, Agnes! Don't say that. If we don't stop this, in five hundred years we are going to be a mongrel race."

"What difference does it make to you? You don't have any children, and we'll certainly all be gone in a hundred years."

When I saw the shock on Bob's face, I put my hand on his and said, "I told you, didn't I?"

I certainly knew that the prejudices of my childhood were alive and well. When Birdy left us to approach another group with her dreadful solicitation, it compounded my determination to eventually tackle the subject of racism on television.

From the happy days with my mother and Aunt Emma, we went on to Chicago. Although my father was not very welcoming, Hazel was glad to see us because he hadn't brought her to the wedding. Hazel was intent on having a festive time, despite Harry's awful mood. He sat across from me at dinner at a restaurant and just stared. His face suggested the misery of someone totally rejected, as if he was recalling how I had offended him. Every attempt by Hazel and me to lighten his mood was a total failure.

Suddenly he said, "I'm going home."

I tried to kiss him good-bye, but he wouldn't accept it. I told him I'd stop by to see him the following day. The next morning, we drove to a Chrysler dealership so Bob could have the car checked and talk shop with a dealer he knew. He dropped me off at my father's apartment. Hazel was out visiting her sister.

"Bob isn't going to make it," Harry told me.

"What do you mean? He has an important job at Chrysler Corporation. He just got promoted again."

"No, he doesn't. I've checked him out. You're just wasting your time. You made a mistake marrying him."

Suddenly I broke my promise to myself not to react to his antics. I told him I knew he had called his cousin Mamie in Nashville and told her he had bought me an expensive wardrobe and staged a beautiful wedding for me. He had in fact done nothing. I should have known how he would react to being called a liar.

My father looked right through me and said, "Get out."

I fled. The tears started when I got to Bob in the car. I told him we'd fought because I asked why he was bragging about paying for the wedding when he hadn't done a thing.

Bob tried to console me. "He'll get over it. We can make peace with him."

Knowing my father, I doubted his prediction would come true. I never told Bob what Harry said about him.

The final leg of the journey to Davenport was exactly what we needed after another bad encounter with my father. If my childhood had been fraught, Bob's childhood had been tragic. Bob was born in Brookfield, Wisconsin, and his father,

Dr. Robert Thomas Ashton Nixon, had been one of three brothers, each a respected doctor in a different Wisconsin town. However, his mother died when he was seven, and his father was killed in a train wreck when he was fourteen.

Bob was raised by relatives before enlisting in the navy on the day after Pearl Harbor. When he returned from the war, the Priesters brought him into their tribe. It was just one of the endless examples of how Hank's parents' generosity, especially his dad's unselfishness, was a beautiful counterpoint to my own father's behavior. Thus our visit to Davenport was a homecoming for both of us.

A month after we returned from our travels, I was overjoyed to hear an obstetrician tell me, "You can expect a baby around February 22." The news wiped out the disappointment that remained from the *Search for Tomorrow* disaster. Being pregnant did not lessen my dedication to my career, however. To the contrary, I knew I wanted my success as a mother to be accompanied by my success as a writer. I was able to sell many small stories for *The Kate Smith Hour* while following Dr. Clader's orders scrupulously to ensure a healthy pregnancy.

Ten months after our wedding, I had the most amazing experience of my life. Through a pain-sedated haze, I was aware of the doctors giving orders and my body being moved to a different bed. A nurse came toward me holding a tightly wrapped tiny bit of humanity.

Immediately the haze evaporated, and I was hit with a bolt of love. It was so overwhelming that I was unable to speak. The nurse said, "Here's your baby. Be careful with her." She put the tiny bundle in my arms. I was overcome with joy and let myself drift away with this blissful moment. Suddenly I knew what life was all about.

Right after delivery my obstetrician made sure to warn me,

"You can't count on birth control, you know. If you don't want to get pregnant, don't have sex."

Thanking the doctor, I promised to remember his advice—so it was all of four months before we were pregnant again. Bob was transferred to Syracuse, New York, and in February 1953, we moved into a rented house on Buckingham Avenue with our twelve-month-old, Cathy, and baby number two due in April. Syracuse had lovely people but the coldest weather I had ever experienced. Our house consisted of three bedrooms, a living room, a kitchen, and a dining room. The third floor had our room with a bath; a guest bedroom, which became my studio with a typewriter, typing and carbon paper, yellow legal pads, and pencils; and a third bedroom that we designated as the nursery.

Each day, Bob and I would have breakfast, which I prepared, and then I would nurse the baby. Afterward, she usually fell asleep, and her morning nap afforded an excellent time to begin writing. I was also fortunate that a nice young lady named Neddy helped keep the house clean and often babysat Cathy so I could write.

At times, my determination to keep up with my writing became humorous. I was pleased to get the assignment to write a treatment for a screen adaptation of *Keep Your Head Up, Mr. Putnam*. (A treatment is a short synopsis that executives use to determine if they like the writer's "take.") It was a lot of work for not much pay, so I was thrilled when it led to an assignment for the script adaptation.

However, I had to take a plane to New York City for a story conference. The script was based on a true story about a man who lost his eyesight in a hunting accident. Since he was playing the lead, Robert Montgomery wanted to discuss certain important scenes. I was eight months pregnant with my second baby, so my wardrobe required special attention. The Putnam family was going to be at the story meeting, and I wanted to look my best. I also decided I would keep a coat on the whole time to disguise my condition, because I was pretty sure they wouldn't hire me if I was pregnant. Looking at myself in the mirror, I thought no one would think I was pregnant. That idea was squashed when the stewards at the waiting plane said, "How pregnant are you? If you're eight months, we can't let you on the flight."

I was forced to take the train, so the conference was changed to the next afternoon. The meeting was with Robert Montgomery, Mrs. Putnam, and her son Peter, who wrote the autobiography. I enjoyed meeting them and was able to do what I thought was a good job in eight weeks. It was a bit of a hard deadline. Mary was born the day after I turned in the script, on April 26, 1953.

Nursing two babies required a new game plan. Bob took over breakfast duty and gave the babies their midnight supplemental bottles, which allowed me to devote our midnight shift to writing scripts. That plan worked fine—and it wasn't all work, because a few months later, I greeted Bob with the news that baby number three was on the way.

One evening, in my ninth month, a Chrysler vice president from Detroit was making the rounds, and Bob brought him over for dinner. During dessert, my labor pains started, and I announced that we had to go to the hospital. Fast. Bob turned to his superior and asked if he would be so kind as to stay with the sleeping babies. Bob assured him they would not wake before he got back from dropping me at the hospital. The startled VP agreed, and we rushed off. Bob's joy was boundless when the doctor announced that the baby and I were both healthy and beautiful. The generous and exhausted VP told his own version of that evening's events:

"It seemed an eternity before a friendly neighbor who Agnes called arrived to take over. It was well past my bedtime when I got to my hotel. Just as I fell into a hard-earned sleep, the telephone rang."

It was an effervescent Bob. "I had to call. I knew you wouldn't go to sleep until you got the news. It's a boy!"

# Chapter 13

# THE TIES THAT BIND

Taking care of our three children made writing almost impossible. Since we couldn't afford full-time help, I worried that I needed to put my career on hold for a little while. Bob came to me and said, "I'm feeling terrible seeing you work so hard and getting up from short naps to take care of the children."

I replied, "I could take five years off and then go back to writing."

Bob said, "Honey, it's ridiculous to give it up. It means too much to you. I'll do more with the kids. You're doing great. Do you really think you could take a break and then go back?"

Bob knew how much writing meant to me and hated to see me give up my career. I was devastated by the idea of not writing, but the sporadic assignments took an enormous amount of time to complete, and the bottom line was that the work didn't even pay enough for someone to help with the kids. It was all just becoming too much. So it was a huge relief when the telephone rang one day and it was Irna Phillips, who told me she had done her Hollywood stint and was moving back to Chicago. But more important, she was developing a new half-hour soap opera, *As the World Turns,* and needed a dialogist to write the lines for *Guiding Light.* She asked if I was available.

Irna and I were such good friends that I confided in her

how serendipitous the offer was. She had saved me from giving up writing, because the full-time job paid much more than the freelance assignments. I could now afford help for my three babies. Irna laughed and said, "Good! Could you just wait 'til I finish my new show before you get pregnant again?"

Another call, this time to Bob, made him the Eastern Seaboard zone manager for Chrysler, which meant we were headed back to Philadelphia. I was so happy to return, but I was not too thrilled when Bob surprised me by buying a house in Havertown without my having seen it.

When I complained, he said, "I knew this wouldn't be your dream house, but I think it will work for now. You can search until you find what you want, and we'll see where that takes us."

My first transition was settling the children into kindergarten and preschool. Since I was gainfully employed as the writer for *Guiding Light,* I set out to find someone who could help me keep my house, cook, and care for the children. Fortunately, I only had to go to Chicago or New York for story meetings with Irna about twice a year. But my writing load was intense. Depending on the complexities of the characters and story, I would write for eight to ten hours a day, Monday through Friday. The weekends were in theory a little better, but when Irna wanted a script, she would often dictate an outline to Rose on Friday. She would call me and sympathize about taking up my weekend, and then recite it to me.

Meanwhile, I was eager to make female friends, and expected to do so through Bob's business and the children's schools. To my dismay, I found the relationship between me and other mothers very different from what I'd enjoyed with other working women in New York. As a working mom with children to raise, I was a curiosity to most of these mothers. It was hard for them to understand that writing a television show took so much of my time away from my children that I often needed to decline the social events they invited me to. Many of them presumed it was impossible for me to be a caring mother.

One day, a woman with whom I was close said to me, "Agnes, I have to say something to you because we are good friends. You cannot be a good mother spending all the time you do working. It's just not fair to your children. If you don't give up the work, your children will suffer."

I was too shocked and hurt to try to change her mind, and after a short time, our friendship ended. Fortunately, I met three women who did not think I was an oddity. One was a doctor of psychiatry, and another was so brilliant that she'd won a scholarship to Vassar College, after which she dedicated her life to raising scholarship funds for others. I also became fast friends with a delightful woman who was raising three children and who understood and embraced my need to be both a writer and a mother.

Sometimes, being a writer who was also a mother played out in ways I didn't expect. On February 6, 1957, near midnight, my oldest daughter, Cathy, was two weeks shy of her fifth birthday. Mary was almost four, Bobby was two and a half, and Emily was about to be born. Bob was signing me in at Bryn Mawr Hospital's maternity ward. I lay in bed timing my contractions as the doctor instructed. The door flew open and a young nurse entered.

"Good evening, Mrs. Nixon. My name is Ginger, and I'm your night nurse. But since you're having a baby, wouldn't you rather be on the delivery floor?" She seemed to be overflowing with energy and enthusiasm.

After a formidable contraction subsided, I said, "No. I have long labors. I don't want to waste the time."

"How long did your previous labor last?" Ginger asked.

"Fifty-two hours."

"Oh, my goodness. My sister had a baby, and she didn't even get to the hospital in time. He was born in the car. She had to wrap him up in her coat. But he was just fine. Lucky, wasn't she?"

"Mm," I commented.

Ginger now noticed my small suitcase on the bedside table.

"Oh, you haven't unpacked. I love to see the sweet little things mothers bring for their newborns to wear home. I'll put them away for you."

But when she lifted the lid of the case, instead of baby clothes she saw a lump of shiny gray metal. She jumped back with a loud gasp. "Is that a machine gun?" she asked.

With momentary control of my breath, I explained, "Dictaphone. I talk into it, and it records the lines of dialogue for my show." The joy of discovery filled Ginger's face.

"Oh, you're that woman who writes soap operas, aren't you? Of course! I knew the name was familiar. You write *The Guiding Light*? That's one of my favorites. I used to watch it with my grandmother. I loved Bert Bauer and her son, Mike, and Julie, of course. I hope Julie and Mike get back together soon. He really loves her, you know. But Julie has been a little bitchy lately, don't you think? Are you going to get them back together? Oh, I know I shouldn't ask you that, but you're amazing. The chart says that this is your fourth baby. Is that true?"

"True," I gasped through clenched teeth.

"Well, that's just amazing. Writing a soap opera and four children! It blows my mind. How do you do it? I mean, how do you—"

The intensity of the latest contraction was a welcome signal. As my body tried to flow with it, I interrupted Ginger. "Forget it. Page Dr. Clader quick; it's showtime."

Later that day, as I sat in a comfortable chair nursing my new daughter, Emily, I looked out at the garden and the golden sky. Sunset has always been my favorite time of day. Gratitude swept over me. I realized how lucky I was. I had a wonderful husband, four seraphic children, and a job as head writer of *Guiding Light,* which provided me with enough income to cover help with household chores and laundry expenses. I had everything I could possibly want—or did I? *Guiding Light* had shown me that I could tell all kinds of stories and tackle all sorts of social issues—and I was just getting started.

Shortly after I returned home, my close friend Anne Morris broke the news that her husband and our dear family friend, John Hickenlooper, had stomach cancer. Hick was thirty-eight, and they, too, were in the midst of raising four children. It was a cruel blow and an awful ordeal for the family. He suffered so much that I wanted to do a story about cancer in some way that might help others.

After Hick died, I started to do some research and learned there was no cure or known preventative measures for what had felled this wonderful husband, father, and friend. However, the doctors pointed out that uterine cancer was curable if caught in time by an easy Pap test, but few women were having one. I knew right then that *Guiding Light*'s beloved Bert Bauer would discover she had cancer after not getting a Pap test for years. The show's sponsors approved the idea, but it did not go so easily with the network.

One CBS exec said, "No, no, no. This is an entertainment show. You can't talk about cancer."

I pushed back, but the men in the room resisted mightily and their attitude irritated me. When they finally relented, I was forbidden from using *cancer, uterus,* or *hysterectomy* in the dialogue.

I was so mad that I wrote a long-term story projection in which Bert's son, Michael, who was working in South America, came home because his mother was having surgery. The audience was so interested in Michael's getting back with Julie that I knew once I got it started, CBS couldn't stop the story. After all, life is soap: the real world keeps coming at you.

So Bert went to the doctor for a physical and was asked, "How long since you have had a Pap test?"

"Oh, I don't even remember. I've been so busy," she responded.

The screening discovered the irregular cells, and Bert's on-air response to her doctor was, "Whatever happens to me, I'm going to tell all my friends not to make the mistake I did."

Viewers were deeply engaged in Bert's medical troubles, and the ratings never suffered. My own doctor said so many women came in for tests that he started asking why. The answer was always the same: "I came because Bert Bauer said I should."

After living through Hick's tragic death, bringing possibly the first cancer story to the air was wonderfully satisfying. Seeing the good it did helped to plant the seed of ambition about starting something that was mine. I began to dream of fewer suits standing in my way. If I had my own show, maybe I wouldn't have to use stealth tactics to get progressive story lines on the air.

But I also had doubts: Would it be foolish to listen to the voices in my head suggesting a plot that could turn into a serial drama? Should I simply realize how fortunate I was and be content? The debate continued in my mind until the real question emerged: Could I close the door and shut out all those appealing dreams?

As usual, I discussed it with Bob.

With his lovable smile, he said, "I was wondering when we would get to this point. When I was pushing marriage, I told you that I knew writing was part of who you are and that I love all of you. So I think we will just face it together."

"Even with four children? Even though you'll have to give up some of your golf games?" I asked. "Even then?"

"Even then," he said.

And so, at the cost of some very desirable golf games, we soldiered on with his good nature and dedication to our partnership. Soon after that conversation, I woke to find a cartoon taped to my dressing-table mirror, showing a woman with curlers in her hair sound asleep in bed and a man holding a screaming baby in his arms. Under the picture the man was saying, "Nobody ever asked me how I could combine marriage and a career."

I thought I would dissolve in laughter and appreciation.

BEING A WORKING mom wasn't always smooth sailing, however. A few memorable incidents come to mind. One Halloween morning as I was cooking breakfast, the sight of my son, Bobby, made me spill the hot chocolate. His face was as large and puffy as the pumpkin, and horribly blistered. I said, "Bobby, what happened?" He insisted nothing was wrong, that he felt just fine, but his expression indicated differently. While Bob served breakfast to the girls, I bundled Bobby into the car and rushed over to our pediatrician. After removing quite a few red pellets from Bobby's face, the doctor told me that the material was wax. Then the truth came out.

Halloween eve, Bobby had gotten the idea of making a mask so that he could go into his sisters' room and frighten them. So he'd gone down to the pantry, found the ends of some red candles I had used the previous Christmas, put them into a saucepan, and started to melt them. However, when he'd leaned down to inspect the bubbling wax, it had exploded in his face, embedding the wax bits in his skin. We were lucky more damage wasn't done.

Then there was our vacation to St. Croix. Bob was unable to join us, so I was there with the four kids and no help. Sitting on the ocean's edge, the girls and I were waiting for Bobby to join us. When he didn't, I asked if anyone had seen him. A man walking by told me that he had seen a young boy about ten years old all alone in a canoe far out on the sea. I stared at an empty canoe far out on the waves, trembling with anxiety, terrified that I'd never see my son again. What would I say to Bob? More than an hour later, Bobby's head popped from under the water. When I saw him, I said, "Bobby Nixon . . . are you all right? Where have you been?"

Bobby's eyes were wide with wonder. "Skin diving!" he exclaimed.

"Skin diving? Why? We thought you had drowned. Why didn't you tell me?"

"Mom, it's just unbelievable down there."

"Where is 'down there'?"

"The coral reef. Tropical fish are everywhere. I'm sorry, Mom. I couldn't take my eyes off them. Can I go back in?"

"Absolutely not. You stay right here with us. We're going to dinner soon."

"Please let me go in the morning."

"You scared me to death. I'll give you my answer after I speak to your father."

"I can't wait to tell Dad what I saw. I'll never forget it. . . . You're not mad at me, are you?"

Bobby was so enthralled that he couldn't even fathom my

terror. And he never did forget the way he felt that day. Bobby's fascination with the sea and wildlife led him to a remarkable career creating Academy Award–nominated and Emmy Award–winning films about the ocean and how our lives depend on it.

Cathy, my eldest, was also responsible for a few major scares. The first was when she was only thirteen months old and Mary was a newborn in a crib. During my postpartum exam after Mary's birth, the doctor recommended that I take a little Ex-Lax, which I bought in the drugstore on the way home. I broke off a small piece, which I ate, and then I put the rest in my pocketbook. On returning to our house, I put Cathy in her playpen and threw my purse on the chair, two feet away from the playpen. I went upstairs to see if Mary needed nursing, telling the sitter to fix some porridge for Cathy and to frequently check on her.

Fifteen minutes later, a very disturbed sitter called me to come down. In the short time I had been upstairs, by some acrobatic maneuver Cathy had managed to inch the playpen over to the chair and reach into my pocketbook. It was now wide open on the floor of the playpen with the contents spread out. The Ex-Lax package was open, and her satisfied little face was covered with chocolate. How had she even realized my purse had something that looked like candy in it? When I called the pediatrician, he instructed us to go to the hospital right away.

I called Bob, who rushed home to go with me. Our baby had to have a tube put down her stomach. Bob pleaded with the ER doctor to let him stay and hold Cathy, to no avail. We could hear her screaming from the waiting room. Bob previously had a stomach ulcer, but it had gone away. That afternoon, however, we had to stop at a drugstore to get some ulcer medicine. Luckily, Cathy was fine after they got the laxatives out.

Another day, while I was trying to select a wallpaper pattern with the paperhanger in the living room, the children were eating breakfast cereal at the kitchen table—or so I thought. Cathy noticed that, in the open cabinet over the stove, there was a box of her favorite dried apricots. She pulled a step stool up to the stove and climbed to retrieve the apricots, unmindful of the saucepan of eggs that was brimming with boiling water. When I heard her scream, I knew what had happened. I rushed her to the doctor, who bandaged her third-degree burn. Each morning for three weeks, I took her to the doctor's office for special ointment and bandages, all while blaming myself for leaving the apricots where Cathy could see them.

Other instances were more endearing than hair-raising. The headboard of Bobby's bed was so crammed with stuffed animals that they had to be removed in order to make the bed. One stuffed squirrel was particularly lifelike. When I picked it up, it dashed from my hand and headed toward the window . . . because it was a *live* squirrel. It had been pushed out of its nest and had landed on a ledge near Bobby's bedroom window, where it found a safe haven. Bobby named it Ivan, fed it with a medicine dropper, and kept it in his jacket pocket.

Finally, the inevitable day came, and it was time for the squirrel to go back where he belonged. Bobby took it to the maple tree and showed it how to climb. I still cherish the memory of that little nine-year-old sadly watching the squirrel jump from limb to limb in pursuit of his destiny, waving and telling it to have a good life.

Mary was the quintessentially affable second child, offset by a year-older sister who was outspoken about her likes and dislikes. One evening, an aunt of mine was dining with us, and she complimented Cathy on the dress she was wearing. Cathy complained that she hated it. Mary joyfully announced, "It will be mine next year!"

Sometimes the two of them conspired against me. Once, I had to take them to the pediatrician's office for booster shots. After Cathy got her shot, she said indignantly, "That hurt. You're not going to do that to my Mary." She leaned through the doorway and called out, "Run, Mary, run!" Mary took off, screaming her lungs out. She didn't know what she was afraid of, but she was totally terrified. Around and around she went, with Cathy joining in, both children screaming. The doctor and his receptionist had to help me corral them and quickly administer the booster to Mary. When we got home, I found that Bobby was crying. He had stepped on a nail that pushed through his sneaker and into his foot.

On seeing us enter his office a second time, the doctor asked prosaically, "Are you here again, or still here?"

DURING THIS TIME, with so many wonderful memories of my own children, I always harbored thoughts, as I so often had, about what opportunity I could create to reconcile with my father. Nine years had passed since I had last seen him, on our post-wedding trip to Chicago. He hadn't met any of his grandchildren, let alone spoken to them. I wrote him letters about them and sent copious pictures, saying how I yearned for them to get to know their grandfather. But I never heard a word from the man who could not forgive me for trying to force him to sell his business.

My father had smoked four packs of cigarettes a day for decades but quit after his heart attack at fifty-seven. Seven years later, in March of 1958, my father and Hazel were spending the winter at their home in Palm Beach. The telephone rang and I heard Bob say, "Well, hello, Hazel."

I was so happy because I thought my father might talk to me, that my letters and pictures of the children had finally worked.

When Bob said, "Yes, Ag is right here . . . Oh. When did it happen?" I knew my father was gone. I took the phone and Hazel simply said, "We've lost him." She explained, "We came home from dinner and he started playing with his little dog. I went to turn down our bed. When I came out, he was sitting on the floor with the dog in his lap. I walked over and said, 'Harry, stop playing with the puppy. Come on to bed.' I put my hand on his shoulder and he just rolled over. He was gone. His doctor said it was a massive heart attack."

Bob and I left on a plane for Chicago. I told him Hazel was having a difficult time bringing Harry home. His two best friends were the leading morticians in Chicago, and typical of Harry, he had promised each of them that they would "get the job" when he passed on. Finally realizing it was "classic Harry," they settled the dispute with laughter and agreed to share "the job."

The funeral was set for the next morning at ten o'clock, and Bob and I made our reservation to return that afternoon. After everyone left the viewing at the funeral home, they gave us a little room where Hazel and I could talk uninterrupted. Hazel said, "If we had just had another few weeks, I think it would have all been fine, because he really did love you and the children."

I'm afraid I doubted Hazel. "Did he say that?" I asked.

Hazel replied, "Yes, he did. . . . You know the Kodak pictures you sent to him?"

My voice betrayed my eagerness. "What about them?"

"He would sit at his desk with a magnifying glass, studying the face of every child. Last Christmas, he pointed to one picture and said, 'That little Cathy looks like Agnes when she used to call me Daddy.'"

Overcome with sadness, I looked at Hazel and begged her to tell me more. Hazel said that she had replied, "For the love of God, Harry, let me call Agnes so you can make peace, so you can have the children spend some time with us in the summer." He'd said, "No, I'll get to love them and something will happen, and they will be taken away from me."

"I was afraid to call you, Agnes," Hazel shared. "He said if I did, he would never forgive me. I wish now I had."

"I know," I said. "It would be like before. I would do something that would tick him off, and he would get so mad and there was nothing I could do."

"It's just so sad. I tried everything I could."

I put my arms around her. "Thank you so much for telling me."

My father's secretary joined us and said to me, "Your father's lawyer wants you in his office tomorrow morning before the service."

"For what?" I asked.

She didn't know but said it was important for me to be there.

The next morning, we entered the lawyer's private office, and he took out my father's will. Before he gave it to us, he said he needed to share some context. "You know, your father was a very successful businessman. He has provided for Hazel so she can live comfortably without worry. Agnes, although your father did not leave you anything, he left the rest of his estate to your four children to provide for their education. He did name you executor of their trust. That means you will decide where they go to school."

As my tears started to flow, Bob put his arm around me and said, "Come on, honey. We have to get to the funeral home. We have to get in the procession."

Arriving at the funeral home, I asked Bob to wait. I dashed out of the car, past the doorman.

"Please, don't close the coffin yet!"

Harry looked so small and vulnerable. My tears began. I leaned toward him and whispered, "I'm sorry I couldn't find a way to ease your pain. I love you and know you loved my children. I promise they would have loved you."

I leaned over and kissed his forehead.

"*Requiescat in pace.* . . . Rest in peace. I love you, Daddy."

# Chapter 14

# PINE VALLEY DREAMS

My father's death had a dramatic effect on my writing style. I made it a practice to be more reflective about everything I was working on and to describe experiences I'd had in my own personal life, including my past with Harry.

In addition, I became increasingly aware that my narrative bent was different from that of the other serial dramas on the air. I had always felt the older serials centered on interpersonal conflicts: jealousy, hate, love, or avarice. Any of these can, indeed, create dramatic tension, but I wanted to do more with my scripts. I wanted to show the causes of the tragedy that beset humankind. The trauma of my shattered family made me want to explore whether many of the world's problems were caused not only by the emotions of one person but by outside circumstances. I was searching for recovery for myself.

Along the way, I met Freddie Silverman, the CBS director of daytime programming. When I was dialoging *Guiding Light,* we both attended all story readings, and his enthusiasm for the stories and the actors made an impression. Freddie never hesitated to give his opinion, good or bad, about anything. At times, Freddie and Irna would disagree about a certain story line, and their arguments would become pretty heated. While Irna would sometimes reject his ideas, often they would come up with a brilliant solution together. It seemed to me that they had a mother-son relationship, and Irna was clearly fond of him—but she also knew she had the final say.

Freddie's interest in writers was as strong as his interest in story, and he often encouraged me to write a show of my own. I admitted it was a dream of mine. He was indefatigable in urging me to keep at it, insisting he would help me get it on the air. Therefore, I felt if I ever needed a friend, I had one at CBS.

Deciding on the subject matter of a soap opera, however, is not as easy as you might think. My studio floor was littered with bits of paper with possibilities jotted on them, but none of them contained a problem that would involve a large number of interconnected characters. Then, one day in 1961, a friend told me about something she had observed at a reception at the beautiful home of a well-to-do couple. The hostess had been her husband's secretary, and of course there had been a lot of gossip about that. While the party was in full swing, the doorbell rang and the hostess answered. She opened the door to a beautiful teenage girl who said, "Mother!"

The hostess said, "I told you never to come here again," and then she slammed the door in the girl's face. My friend didn't know what happened after that, but she was struck by the odd scene.

After thinking about that situation for a few hours, I knew I had my plot. But in my reconstruction, the young woman became a young man, and many other aspects were changed. These are the main characters of *All My Children,* plus the backstory that brought them to the opening of the show. When Amy Parker's parents died, her sister Ruth took on a maternal role. Then, when Amy was seduced and impregnated by a conscienceless Nick Davis, Ruth—who was married to a football star named Ted Brent and childless—came up with the perfect solution for Amy. "The baby's due in September. You'll come live with us while Ted is at training camp, and I'll say I had the baby."

As I thought about the characters in more depth, the plot unspooled naturally, and I wrote the following outline:

A few years later, Amy finished secretarial school and was employed by a lawyer, Lincoln Tyler, who married her. He was the son of Dr. Charles Tyler, chief of staff of Pine Valley Hospital, and his socially prominent wife, Phoebe Tyler, who believed their son had married beneath him. One night, Ted Brent, after scoring the winning touchdown for his team, drank too much while celebrating with teammates. He wrecked his car, and the resulting back injury prevented him from ever playing football again. As the show opens, Ted Brent sits at his desk in a used-car lot, an embittered man.

During the ensuing years, Ruth Brent has raised Amy's son, Philip, as her own child and watched, adoringly, as he's grown into a handsome, athletic teenager. She thinks of him solely as her son, rarely as her nephew. Amy, on the other hand, having borne no children with Lincoln, yearns to find an outlet for the undeniable love she has for Philip (the truth of Philip's parentage is a complete secret in Pine Valley).

Newly returned to Pine Valley, Dr. Joseph Martin now lives with his widowed mother, Grandma Kate, and has brought his son, Jeff, and his daughter, Tara. Dr. Tyler arranged his position at Pine Valley Hospital.

Charles Tyler's son, Charles Jr., was Joseph's best friend in high school and medical school, and his other son, Chuck, is a close friend of Philip's. But the imperious Phoebe Tyler would prefer her beloved grandson have a more prestigious friend.

Meanwhile, a chastened Nick Davis has returned to Pine Valley, regretting abandoning Amy and wanting to make amends and see what happened to their child. Knowing how close they were, Nick Davis goes first to Amy's sister, Ruth, with his regrets about his past behavior. Ruth tells him that the baby was a girl and was put up for adoption, and that they have no idea where she is.

Another volatile scene occurs when Ruth tells Nick Davis to stay away from Amy, because she's happily married to Lincoln Tyler. However, Nick is still curious. On a day when he knows her lawyer husband is in court, Nick knocks on Amy's door. Amy is able to keep her composure while Nick says how sorry he is for the way he treated her in the past. But now he wants to know what happened to their child. That's when Amy loses it and tells him that it's none of his business, to go away and leave her alone. Amy's extreme reaction causes Nick to suspect something, but Nick thinks she is nervous because her rich in-laws don't know that she had a baby.

Amy latches on to that excuse, and she tells him to leave her alone and to leave Pine Valley. But to Amy's frustration, he can't really do that, because a friend of his has opened ballroom-dancing studios in New York City and Philadelphia, and he has come here to open a branch studio in Pine Valley.

Meanwhile, close friends Philip Brent and Chuck Tyler like the same sports and the same books, and not surprisingly, they both fall in love with the same girl when Tara Martin moves to Pine Valley with her father. Because Phil and Tara are both so fond of Chuck, they try to keep from him the fact that Tara returns Philip's love.

The one main character who has not been mentioned is a high school student—the beautiful, self-indulgent, and determined-to-get-her-way Erica Kane. Probably the greatest motivator in Erica's life is the fact that her father abandoned her mother, Mona, and her to follow his career as a movie producer in Hollywood. But Erica never admits that fact. Rather, she blames his flight on Mona, who stoically accepts Erica's criticism that she was an inadequate wife.

There is one person who castigates Erica for her treatment of her mother: Mona's dear friend Nick Davis. Their friendship goes back to when Nick, a failing math student, was tutored by Mona until he was finally able to graduate. Nick's constant criticism of Erica will later inflame many scenes between them in ensuing episodes, and will present the audience with important past events of all these major characters.

As I created these backstories for my show during the summer of 1963, the children and I spent ten days with Aunt Emma and Mother in Nashville. One day we went to Centennial Park, and Mother took the kids cane-pole fishing and played Mother, May I? with them. It was just a lovely day, but I noticed something was different with her. Every now and then, she was challenged by a routine task, such as combing her long hair and fastening it into a bun.

Then, at Christmas, Aunt Emma and Mother came for their usual visit, and Mother had trouble walking up the stairs. When I asked her if she was feeling well, she just said that she needed more exercise. When Aunt Emma confirmed the problem, I made up an excuse to go to Nashville.

Dr. Chucker, our longtime family doctor, simply said, "Agnes, did you expect her to be twenty years old for the rest of your life? Come on, join the seniors' club."

In the past, Aunt Emma, sixteen years older and with her short leg, had needed support from Mother. But by the time of our visit, Mother's mobility was so bad that she was now relying on her elder sister. Heartbroken, Emma explained to me she could no longer physically take care of Mother. She was struggling to help her in and out of the bathtub. I began to make arrangements to take over. I told Mother she had to come for a long vacation to Philadelphia, where she could see a fine doctor. That was what she thought she was doing, but I knew the time would come when I would have to tell her she was never going home to Nashville. She had a battery of tests at Pennsylvania Hospital, and the doctors broke the news that she had amyotrophic lateral sclerosis, which was commonly known as ALS, or Lou Gehrig's disease.

We got Mother a small apartment, furnished it, and found a nice companion for her. One day, however, a neurologist gave her a medication that she had an allergic reaction to. She started getting jaundice and had to be admitted to Bryn Mawr Hospital. I knew she was suffering—not physically, but mentally. Here was an independent woman who ran the books at a small insurance company, now having to depend on others.

Still, she never complained. She was a stalwart soul who never asked for sympathy and whose only joy in life was bringing joy to those she loved. She slipped away from us on the morning of September 24, 1964. I still feel guilty because I knew she would have preferred it if she had never left Nashville.

I found refuge in returning to work on my idea for a new drama. Before I thought of the name of the show, I felt a need to find a theme for the series.

I tried to think about who the show would be about. I sat down at my typewriter, and the words just appeared on the page . . .

> The great and the least
> The weak and the strong
> The rich and the poor
> In sickness and health

In joy and sorrow
In tragedy and triumph
You are All My Children

This was another case in which I felt I was channeling my Irish ancestors. When I got to the last of the seven lines, I knew that *All My Children* would be the title of the series.

COMING UP WITH the fleshed-out version of my outline—which we in the industry called the "bible" of the series—was not so effortless. It took me a full year after Mother's death, making it five years in total since I had begun formulating the idea. The whole family rejoiced when I wrote the last line. The children said we should have a celebration. Bob reminded us that we had talked about taking a vacation during Christmas, but he explained that his new Chrysler dealership meant he couldn't leave during the holiday.

Bob said that since I needed to edit the whole bible of *All My Children,* he'd spoken to a travel agent who had suggested I take the children to St. Croix. There was a family-type resort with full-time lifeguards, which meant I wouldn't have to supervise the children all by myself and would be able to work. The five of us flew to the islands on the day after Christmas, leaving Bob behind to take care of his new showroom.

The resort, St. Croix by the Sea, was ideal for us. We had our own small bungalow on the beach with quick access to the azure sea, and a kitchen and pantry to make our breakfasts and lunches. The staff kept an eye on the children, so I could sit on the veranda and finish editing the *All My Children* bible while enjoying the warm Caribbean sunlight. I took a break to take the children on a catamaran to snorkel the coral reef at

Wherever I was as a child, dialogue and plot lines for my paper dolls swirled in my head.

Mother was Agnes.
I was little Aggie.

Harry, my tortured father.

I treasured every
minute at St. Mary's.
If I could have paid
for it, I would have
stayed in school
forever.

At Northwestern
with Hank, my
All-American.

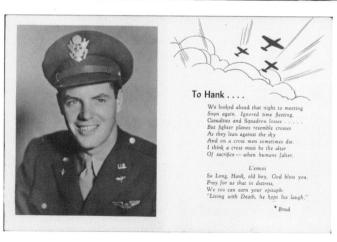

To Hank . . . .

We looked ahead that night to meeting
Soon again. Ignored time fleeting,
Casualties and Squadron losses . . . . .
But fighter planes resemble crosses
As they lean against the sky
And on a cross men sometimes die.
I think a cross must be the altar
Of sacrifice — when humans falter.

L'envoi

So Long, Hank, old boy. God bless you.
Pray for us that in distress,
We too can earn your epitaph:
"Living with Death, he kept his laugh."

* Brud

Our private hero.

Irna Phillips—the mother of us all.

Writing for Irna and *Freedom of Opportunity* expanded my radio reach from across campus to across the country. I loved writing and working with so many smart people— like FDR Jr.

Married! To Bob Nixon, my best man.

When Bob proposed, he said, "Of course you will have a career and a family, because I'll help."

The stars of my real world.

The stars of my "real world of make-believe" on the *One Life to Live* set.

A loud hosanna for Sadie and Joseph Gay, who truly raised the kids with us. Here I'm in the playroom, asking Sadie if I could name a character in my civil rights story line in her honor.

A brilliant actress, Lillian Hayman infused a profound humanity into the role of Sadie Gray, Carla's estranged mother.

I fought to populate my shows with multiple generations, races, and religions, because I knew that diversity and authenticity would arm me with a powerful weapon for social change: beloved characters struggling on opposite sides of a polarizing issue. In 1970, I made Pine Valley homemaker Amy Tyler a strident Vietnam War protester and lured Rosemary Prinz, daytime's biggest star, to *All My Children* to play her.

Throughout my career, I was inseparable from my Dictaphone. I had to get my ideas down whenever and wherever inspiration struck.

I tricked him into buying it, but Bob quickly forgave me. He loved Pine Cottage.

Dropping in on my Pine Valley family.

When Barbara Walters said, "She is the first writer and the first woman to receive this rarely presented Trustees Award," I wondered why I didn't know the person she was talking about.

Blessings to our wonderful fans, who inspired our remarkable company of actors and paid many a tuition bill across forty-one years.

Susan Lucci and I have always had a special bond.

Being honored with the lifetime achievement Emmy was humbling, overwhelming, and really fun.

Erika Slezak is a true talent and a dear friend.

The best part of winning the award was being surrounded by my whole real-world family. For Bob, an orphan at age fourteen, and me, an only child of divorced parents, there was never a moment's doubt: our children and their growing families were our grandest production.

Buck Island. It was so breathtakingly beautiful that President Kennedy had just protected it as the world's first underwater national park.

It was a glorious six days—Bobby's skin-diving excitement aside—that ended all too quickly. The next Saturday, we packed our luggage. I had just put the edited bible on the bottom of a very large Gucci suitcase when Bobby entered, pushing a wheelbarrow of empty conch shells.

"What are you going to do with those?" I asked.

"I'm taking them home," he said.

"You can't," I said. "There's no room."

"I can take them in your totes."

"There wouldn't be room for my books. You have to leave them here."

"Mom, please. I'm going to sell them to my friends for a dollar apiece," Bobby pleaded. "Please, Mom, let me take them home."

When I saw his chin start to quiver, my resolve disintegrated.

"Okay. Get all the sand out of those shells and help me pack these books and everything else in the luggage. It will be a miracle if we can fit everything in, and let's not forget the madras jacket we bought for your dad."

We said good-bye to St. Croix and the taxi took us to the airport, where we were told that our original flight connecting from Puerto Rico to Philadelphia had been canceled because of engine trouble, and we would be put up overnight at a hotel in San Juan. I was wearing a faded madras shirt I had bought five years earlier from the Bryn Mawr Thrift Shop and carrying a camel-hair coat from my first pregnancy. The children were wearing island attire that was badly in need of laundering. Our dress for departure was based on arriving in Philadelphia, and as we entered the El San Juan Hotel casino, women with beehive hairdos looked at us askance. Nevertheless, we had a lovely suite and the meals were delicious. Still, we were so happy to be back on the plane to Philadelphia the next day.

Bob was waiting for us in the baggage terminal when we arrived. He kept his eyes trained on the carousel as our bags came off one by one. I walked up to him, carrying one of the conch-filled totes. He asked, "Have we got it all?"

"All but one," I said.

"What's that?"

I explained that Bobby's conch shells had necessitated some repacking.

Bob said to me, "Where is the *AMC* bible?"

I said, "In the old big Gucci."

He said, "That's the one that's missing."

Despite all the airline's efforts, it stayed missing for ten desperate weeks.

Five years of work, lost in the air. I was crushed. Nothing seemed to matter. My agent said to me, "Maybe you'll have to start over again."

"Are you crazy? I couldn't possibly. I don't have it in me," I replied.

Then I received a beautiful phone call. "Mrs. Nixon, we found it!"

I felt as if life was worth living again. I stepped out into one of those glorious fall days in New York—the air dry and crisp, the sky cobalt blue. People seemed to share my energy and spirit. Walking from the Lombardy Hotel to the Columbia Broadcasting System headquarters at Fifty-Second Street and Avenue of the Americas, I relished the fact that my world of Pine Valley had been returned to me. I spent the next day making copies and then sent one to my agent. Never again would I have only one copy of something I was working on.

My agent sent the bible to CBS, and a few days later, Freddie Silverman called. "Your agent wanted to deliver this news, but I overruled him. I'm happy to say he has a film offer from the network of twenty thousand dollars for your spectacular story, and we are guaranteeing the three p.m. time slot. You will be replacing the Lever Brothers' show *To Tell the Truth*."

I hung up the phone in happy disbelief and called Bob.

"Congratulations!" he said. "I'm so proud of you."

"I can't believe my luck."

Bob said, "It's not luck. It's hard work and tremendous talent. You deserve everything that is coming your way."

"I could never have done it without your support. I love you so much."

"We have a lot of planning to do. And celebrating."

The other phone rang. "Congratulations, Mrs. Nixon. *Variety* would love to get your reaction to *All My Children* being bought by CBS."

I was shocked that they'd already been informed. "Wow, that was fast. I haven't even caught my breath. . . . Well, I can say that I've dreamed about this story for many years. I'm almost at a loss for words, but I want to say thank you to Freddie Silverman for encouraging me to write my own show, and thank you to CBS!"

"Can you tell us the plot?" the reporter prodded.

"I'm not going to divulge the story, but I believe the audience will feel that our characters are very realistic, that they are people they will empathize with. My hope is that many will feel very close to them and that they will be almost like members of their own family."

"Do you have any comment on the fact that CBS is taking *To Tell the Truth* off the air to put your show on?"

"If they are freeing up the time period, I'm grateful to CBS that they are picking up *All My Children*."

"Mrs. Nixon, you have four children, don't you?"

"Yes, I do."

"Do you foresee keeping up with them might be a problem for you?"

I said, "I hope I can manage that. But I really must hang up now."

"Thank you for talking with me. Good-bye."

After the *Variety* reporter hung up, I heard his question to me: "Do you foresee keeping up with them might be a problem for you?" I suddenly realized that question kept reverberating in my brain. Would I be able to do the work and also be a good wife and mother of the children? The amount of work terrified me.

When Bob got home and came up to the studio where I wrote, I said, "We have to talk."

He sat down beside me and said, "What about, honey?"

All the fears about my being a failure in the most important job that I'd ever had came pouring out of me. I said, "Bob, no matter what I say or do, being your wife and the mother of our four children means the world to me. I consider that to be my most important function on this earth, and if you have any thoughts that taking this job will keep me from fulfilling my role, you must tell me now."

Bob put his arm around me and pulled me close. "Aggie, I've always said that I would help you to be a writer and I knew that it would take the two of us working close together. That is what I know we have to do now, and we will. Do you believe that?"

"Yes, I do." Then I broached the question of whether his friends would ask if I was making more than he did. He replied,

"If some horse's ass asks me that stupid question, he would then cease to be my friend." Then Bob kissed me and said, "I have to go cut the grass. You stay here and see what your Irish ancestors tell you to write."

I looked around my studio and the reality set in. On the wall were framed photos: the one of Hank in his air force uniform that I had first put behind my typewriter at Northwestern, a favorite of Irna, snapshots of friends and loved ones. I sat in my comfy chair and went back to the past and some of the rough times, like when I was let go from *Search for Tomorrow*. I asked myself if I had ever been as happy as I was at this very moment. And I said to myself, "Of course you have. Remember when you were six years old and Fred Stroud showed you all the Sunday funny papers he had saved?" There were stacks of bright colors that I could cut out for my own paper dolls, and so many new stories to make up for Tillie the Toiler. I realized that I had felt the same joy then that I did now.

With a rush of emotion, I knew what I was most thankful about: that I had Bob and our four children. I was indeed lucky. And I realized I wouldn't be doing it all on my own. With the size of our new house, four rambunctious children, and our daunting workloads, Bob and I had agreed that we wanted to find a domestic couple who might be willing to pitch in with us.

Mr. and Mrs. Joseph Gay were the first and last applicants we interviewed. They asked us to call them Sadie and Joseph, and they told us they grew up together in the small town of Ahoskie, North Carolina. They owned their own home in Germantown but were looking for a full-time, live-in engagement where they could work together. We felt a connection, and they moved into our home, Pine Cottage, for five days a week. From the beginning, we were more than employer and employee, and soon we were family. They never had children, and loved and helped raise ours as their own. I even promised Sadie that if I ever had my own show, I'd name a character after her. I gratefully acknowledged that without Sadie and Joseph, I would not have had my career as a writer. Beyond that, each of us was deeply enriched by their graceful souls. As I reflected on the opportunity in front of me, I realized how fortunate I was to have them in my life.

And in that moment I also realized, *Oh my, it's Sadie and Joseph's long weekend off, and I promised the kids I would cook spaghetti. It's Bobby's favorite.* I took one more satisfied look around my studio, and then I rushed downstairs and started on the sauce.

ON MONDAY, Freddie Silverman and my William Morris agent, Tony Fantozzi, were waiting for me at the Down Under, a chic, pricey restaurant on the ground floor of the CBS Building. The story goes that when the imposing edifice was planned, CBS president William Paley's wife, Babe—the ultimate paragon of beauty, fashion, and social prominence—suggested he include a pleasant but simple restaurant where employees could enjoy a delicious meal at a sensible price. To date, not a single member of the working class Mrs. Paley wanted to help had been able to afford a meal there.

On joining Freddie and Tony, I asked how Lever would react to the loss of their *To Tell the Truth* franchise. They explained that *Truth* was getting such poor ratings, they had to expect it. "It's the law of the jungle, Aggie," said Fred. "Lever has already been informed of *Truth*'s demise."

Hearing that news rid me of my last concerns about displacing such a well-known program, and I turned my attention to the epicurean menu. Freddie looked at his watch and hurriedly left the table. "I'm due for a meeting with Mr. Paley right now."

"What for?" Tony asked.

"Oh, it's just routine stuff," Freddie explained. "New union rules and information to affiliate stations about *All My Children*. I'll be back in fifteen minutes. Wait for me."

Tony elaborated on what it meant to start a new daytime serial on CBS—the most successful of the three big studios in town—while I prayed silently that I would be able to make *All My Children* a success. I wanted to create a show not only to entertain, but to help people better understand themselves. When Tony saw Freddie returning, his excitement reached new heights.

"What did he say? Is he excited? What did he tell you? Speak!" Tony yelled.

A waiter was passing with a tray of martinis; Freddie grabbed one and drank it down, then looked Tony in the eye and spoke one word: "Dead."

"Mr. Paley? You mean Mr. Paley died?" Tony asked.

Freddie shook his head. "The show has been dropped."

"What the hell are you talking about?" Tony asked.

Freddie answered, "Lever is threatening to sue us for collusion. We can't risk it."

"Collusion? What the fuck is collusion?" Tony demanded.

Freddie tried to explain that collusion was an agreement between two or more persons that could deceive, mislead, or defraud others of their legal rights. Lever Brothers could sue CBS and P & G for committing a violation of the federal antitrust laws.

"That's a bunch of crap," Tony said. "They're bluffing. They haven't got a leg to stand on. You go tell Mr. Paley that."

"I want to keep my job," said Freddie.

"Okay, asshole. I'll go tell him myself!" Tony yelled, obviously thinking about the money he would have made in commissions. When Tony started to leave, Freddie blocked him with a chair. Tony armed himself with a small table, and the fight escalated. As they attracted more attention and the maître d' rushed over, I quickly left.

Mindless of my suitcase at the hotel, I walked in a daze to Penn Station and boarded a train home to my family. All my hopes and dreams about *All My Children* had turned to ashes. In my mind, I heard my father's voice ridiculing my claim to being a writer. I could hear him saying, as he had so many times in the past, "You just don't have what it takes." The question hung in my mind. *Could he be right?* As the taxi drove up our driveway, Bob appeared in the doorway and came to help me out of the backseat.

"What are you doing home from work?" I asked him.

"I came home to be with you," he said. "Lou Weiss called me from William Morris and told me what happened."

"*AMC*'s no good," I said.

"Don't be ridiculous, honey. It's great. It's just the threat of a business lawsuit that scares CBS."

"No. I'm finished. I can see the *Variety* headline: 'Nixon Nixed by CBS.'"

By now we were up in our bedroom, where I took out a copy of the *AMC* bible from my briefcase and put it in the bottom desk drawer.

"Dad was right. I don't have what it takes."

"Will you stop it?" Bob said. "You'll get *Children* on some other network."

"Never. Never!" And with that, I flew into my husband's arms and cried my eyes out.

# Chapter 15

# ONE LIFE TO LIVE

By 1965, it had been twenty-one years since Irna Phillips had hired me as a dialogist. And over those years, we had become very close friends. Although she was much older, there were few women writing for television, and Irna often referred to us as "comrades in arms." So I was not surprised at all when Irna called with some pithy comments about the bad luck I had just suffered with CBS.

"Don't let it get you down, kid," she told me.

"Irna, I feel down and out—really, really out."

"But you'll snap back," she said.

"No, honest, Irna, I don't think I have the guts anymore. I just feel like I'm finished."

In a stern tone, Irna said, "Are you going to let your father win?"

"I don't want him to win, but I don't think I have it in me anymore to write another line."

"You're under a contract to write for *Guiding Light,* aren't you?"

"Of course. I have to do that, and I thank God for it."

"And you have a good associate writer. You can get it done. Piece of cake. All you need, honey, is to get your self-confidence back again, and I know just how you can do it—by becoming the head writer of *Another World.*"

*Another World* was a program on NBC created by Irna quite a few years earlier. She had left the show after an argument with an executive because he refused to move the show to two p.m., where there would be no immediate serial competition. As it stood now, it was going head-to-head with *General Hospital*.

She continued. "I know that's surprising to you, but you know, honey, I stand to make a lot of money from *Another World* if it becomes successful and P & G has to buy it from me. Let me put it this way: if you could save the show, you'd be doing me a tremendous favor."

Realizing that Irna was serious, I became serious myself. "But I haven't watched *Another World* in five years. I was creating *All My Children*."

"So start watching, and I'll ask P & G to send you back years of scripts."

"They wouldn't want me, a writer whose option had been dropped by CBS."

"Not true. I spoke to Procter & Gamble's president, Bob Short. He would love for you to take over. Don't chicken out. Do me this favor."

My husband was tying his shoes before going to work, but I knew he was listening to my conversation. I looked at him questioningly. He said, "Tell her you need a little time to think about it."

I watched the show every day for two weeks. I was shocked by the slow-moving, lachrymose episodes, which almost put me to sleep. I realized that *Another World*'s only hope was to change the plodding pace by adding comedy. Not pranks, but the type of human comedy that we all share. This occurred to me because there were several actors on the show with wonderful comedic talent: Doris Belack, Tony Ponzini, Ann Wedge-worth, Robin Strasser, Judith Barcroft, Constance Ford, and Jordan Charney.

After thinking some more, I decided to accept Irna's offer. I made sure that I'd have the assistance of Hank Priester's sister, Kiki McCabe, who had been my friend since college as well as a dialogist for *Guiding Light*.

With Mother gone, I shared the good news with Aunt Emma, who was always in my thoughts. She had been having some health problems and told me that as she aged, she often prayed that she would die before she had to stop driving her car and going to daily mass. After my mother died, Emma did not want to leave their bungalow, so her youngest sister, Rose, who lived nearby, made sure she had sufficient care. With help, Rose was able to take her to mass. One day after Emma returned from Christ the King Catholic Church, she suffered a stroke.

Toward the end of summer, before the children returned to school, I took the four of them to visit Aunt Emma. She was so grateful for our presence, and she again told her father's stories. The children had heard them countless times before, but they could not get enough of them. We brought some pictures of the children in the dress-up clothes she had made: Cathy as Cinderella, Mary as Tinker Bell, Bobby as Davy Crockett, and Emily as Little Red Riding Hood. When we left, she kissed us good-bye and said to us, "You will always be in my heart, my darlings."

Emma Claire Dalton left us on January 4, 1966. Her family and business associates paid a stirring tribute. Even today, when the Dalton descendants gather, they unfailingly remember her unselfish kindness, how she made their lives so much richer, and how they benefited from her wonderful example. It is not an exaggeration to say that Emma Claire Dalton was our family's private saint.

While I was sad to lose Emma, I knew I had to get back to writing. In my make-believe world, new characters were created—real people with problems. Some of the problems had a comic bent to them, and reviews labeled *Another World* the first soap opera in which humor was a constant. After a year, we'd turned the tables, and *Another World* handily beat ABC's *General Hospital* in the ratings. Without question, that success was what established my track record. And when Irna called to congratulate me on the ratings, she also said that P & G was buying the show. "Thanks for the big favor, kiddo."

That was when the American Broadcasting Company called me.

"Mr. Edward Vane wishes to speak to you," said the woman on the line. "Will you please hold for him?" Like many secretaries who have called me for their bosses, this one spoke with a lilt that gave the impression that she thought she was speaking to a second-class citizen. (Does some secretarial school teach that?) But Ed Vane's jovial greeting made me feel better.

"Congratulations, you really killed us," he said. "May I take you to lunch this week to talk serious business?"

We settled on Friday. After I hung up, my agent, Tony, called to say that Ed Vane told him he was going to contact me, but Ed hadn't given him a chance to call me first. Being a true agent, Tony skipped right to "When are we seeing him?" He then told me they wanted me to do a show for ABC and that I should have an idea ready for Ed. That gave me three days. I had worked for *five years* to develop *All My Children,* allowing for a few family interruptions.

When the day came, I first pitched Ed Vane an idea that I

had always planned to do on *All My Children* if it got on the air. It was a plot exposing the evils of the racial prejudice that had disturbed me during my childhood in the South. My mind raced back to the many times I had sat on a public bus as a little girl and watched black adults pass by me to stand in the crowded rear section, or when I had heard Birdy and others use derogatory words for black people. Now I thought I could use some of those experiences—and my angry feelings about them—for the new show.

Specifically, I took my inspiration from a movie I'd seen some years earlier, *Imitation of Life,* in which a young black woman with a light complexion rejects her race and her mother, causing everyone around her much pain. The movie ends with her attending her mother's funeral full of anguished guilt, re-membering how she caused her mother to suffer. I planned a similar story arc, but with a more upbeat ending that would prompt the audience to examine its own racial prejudices. One of the joys of a daily drama is the luxury of time. To really get people to think, the audience would have to believe that the character was white—which meant I needed all the time I could get.

I decided that the character's name would be Carla Gray, and I created a story about her to fill the next five months. She was engaged to a widowed white doctor named Dr. Jim Craig, but his young daughter, Cathy, did not want him to marry Carla. At the same time, there was a black character named Sadie, who was head of housekeeping for a hospital. (The wonderful actress Lillian Hayman would eventually play Sadie Gray, whose name fulfilled my promise to my house-keeper, Sadie Gay, from years before. Years later, I introduced Lillian and Sadie and they became friends, which was a great thrill for Sadie.)

On the show, Sadie had her own story. We never saw Carla and her in a scene together, and everyone thought Sadie's daughter was dead. Sadie lived in the same apartment building as Anna Wolek, who was also a friend of Carla's. One afternoon, Sadie stopped by Anna's apartment as Carla was walking upstairs. They encountered each other mid-stairway.

Both just stared at each other for a moment, until Sadie said softly, "Clara" (Sadie's name for Carla).

"Mama!" said Clara.

I began my lunch with Ed Vane by telling him the story of Clara meeting her mother, and he exclaimed, "What a Friday ending!" This meant he liked the cliffhanger aspect. The other story I pitched to Ed revolved around a dissociative personality. The idea had sprung from conversations with my dear friend Mary Hansen, the medical doctor and psychiatrist who'd welcomed me as a working mother when she returned to Philadelphia. Mary had answered some pertinent questions about material on *Another World* and *Guiding Light* in the past, and she'd assured me that dissociative identity disorder was a very real problem in our crowded country of fragile egos. Thus was born Victoria Lord, daughter of Victor Lord, a publishing giant who ran the local newspaper, the *Philadelphia Banner,* and insisted that his daughter be named after him to continue his dynasty.

"Don't stop now," Ed Vane said. "Tell me about the other personalities."

I said, "Niki is the opposite of Viki, and that's how the humor comes in."

And then I further set the stage for Ed by explaining how Viki's personalities would come into play, chiefly through the character of Vince Wolek. Vince and his sister, Anna, were seventeen and eighteen when their beloved mother died of cancer. Then, not even two weeks later, their father, whom they adored, died after falling at a construction site at the offices of the *Banner*. Before he died, holding both his children's hands, he told them, "*Liebchen,* take good care of your brother Larry. He's so smart. Make him into somebody."

Anna and Vince promised to honor their father's dying wish. After high school, Anna did her part by taking a secretarial course, which eventually led to a position as a personal secretary to Dr. Tim Craig, a widower and a very prominent doctor at Llanview Hospital. After enjoying many years of a good working relationship, Tim and Anna fell into a warm and loving romantic relationship, which he wanted to culminate in marriage. But Tim's teenage daughter, Cathy, who cherished her close relationship with her father, was opposed to having Anna as a stepmother. Cathy Craig versus Anna would be a very strong element in future plotting.

As for Vince's role in keeping his promise to his father, he took a job driving trucks containing hazardous materials to earn a double salary. The beginning of the serial would have a scene between Vince and his best friend from high school, Bob Scott, a reporter for the *Banner*. In this scene, we learn that Vince ridiculed Bob Scott's love for Victoria Lord, who, in his opinion, was an ice princess.

Vince despised Victoria's wealthy publisher father because Vince blamed Victor for the lax safety regulations that caused his father's death. Victor Lord, on the other hand, supported the building company by blaming the union for putting too few men on the site. The argument between the magnate and the fiery-tempered worker escalated at a public meeting, and the police had to restrain Vince from physically attacking Victor.

When the show opened, Larry Wolek had received his degree from medical school and was working as an intern at Llanview Hospital when he fell in love with a young woman who did charitable work there. The only trouble was that Meredith was Victor Lord's youngest daughter, which drove Larry's brother, Vince, wild and would cause many angry scenes in future stories. Meredith begged Viki to ask Victor to permit them to have a reception for Larry in honor of his becoming a doctor, but Victor was adamantly opposed. So the scene was set for high drama that afternoon, and what happened far surpassed what one might even expect.

After Viki toasted Larry, she sat next to Vince on the only chair available and said, "I know how proud you are of Larry." Vince was about to respond when he realized that the young woman had put her hand over his.

Looking at her with surprise, he saw a vixen's face and heard her say, "Doesn't she make you want to throw up?"

A bewildered Vince said, "Who the hell are you?"

"I'm Viki Lord's better half. I don't get out nearly as much as I want to, but I think you can help me with that. Come on."

Taking his hand, she led him to a corner of the gallery, where she quickly explained the dissociative personality situation and added, "You will help me, won't you, Vince? I will make it worth your while."

With that, she put her arms around him and gave him a passionate kiss.

That, I told Ed Vane, would be the beginning of the show. I also told him that I finally had the perfect title for it: *One Life to Live*. All my life, it had been a passion of mine, a basic truth: we only have one life to live, and we have to try to make the most out of it. As my babies came along, I was even more obsessed with the brevity of life and how little time we have. I wanted to help other people understand how to make our brief candle burn brightly with a light that shines on the path of life.

Ed called me the next week and said, "The network is solidly behind you. We will premiere the show on July 26, 1968." In those days, ABC was called "the half network" by CBS and NBC because it desperately needed a strong daytime lineup to fully compete. They had high hopes for *One Life to Live*. I did, too.

IT'S USUALLY AN exciting time when a premiere is only ten days away. But as we neared the debut for *One Life to Live,* we had a problem: we had not yet cast the part of Carla/Clara. The casting department auditioned actors on both coasts and in Chicago, but with no success. The head of casting explained that when they found an actress with the right pigmentation, she hadn't tested well.

Marshall Karp, the director of daytime, called me to say that the obvious solution was to cast a dark-skinned Latino or Italian woman. He thought that would solve everything. I was adamant that we could not do that. I told him that if we could not find an appropriate actress, we had to drop the story for the time being.

I was frustrated: a published slogan at the time was "Black Is Beautiful," yet we couldn't even cast the part. As I picked up the Sunday edition of the *New York Times,* I was startled to see a beautiful woman's face looking back at me. Her letter to the editor was titled "How Black Do You Have to Be?" The writer was Ellen Holly, a well-known and exceptional talent who had often performed in Shakespearean productions.

As she related her story, it was amazingly similar to Carla's. When Ellen Holly auditioned for a Caucasian part and said she was black, she was dropped from consideration. When she auditioned for a black part, the producers eliminated her because she was too light skinned.

I could not believe it. I called my friend Brandon Stoddard, who was vice president of ABC Daytime. When I identified myself, he said, "I was just about to call you. You saw it, right?" Brandon got through to Ellen that morning and scheduled a meeting for first thing Monday. Ellen was magnificent in the part, and we were excited to have finally found our Carla.

After *One Life to Live*'s successful premiere, I was thrilled to watch the plotlines develop on air in exciting ways, including the Carla/Clara story. A black resident at Llanview Hospital, Dr. Jack Scott, broke their engagement when he learned that she had rejected her race to pass for white. Carla, in turn, was upset with Jack because she felt he didn't know what it meant to be black. He lived a life of comfort because his father was a highly respected judge in Philadelphia, a man modeled after Raymond Alexander. Although many people agreed with Carla, she and Jack never repaired their relationship, and eventually, she met a white police lieutenant, Ed Hall, who worked in juvenile narcotics.

Carla was daytime's first black heroine, and the show about the interracial relationship aired in 1968. Later that year I had Carla and Ed kiss on the air in another soap opera first (Nancy Sinatra and Sammy Davis, Jr.'s kiss had been a television first a year earlier). ABC Standards and Practices gave me the news that the affiliate station in Austin, Texas, got so many protest letters about the interracial relationship that the managers took *One Life to Live* off the air. I thought those viewers needed the message more than anybody, and I hoped they would get it. After a forceful protest from viewers who loved the show, *One*

*Life to Live* returned to the Austin market several weeks later. It was a tremendous personal victory for someone who'd ridden the segregated buses in Nashville as a young girl and watched with dismay as a distinguished elderly black man or woman would walk by the empty "white" seats in the front to stand in the back.

I also received a letter from a man in Seattle, Washington, who wrote: "I protest that white woman kissing that black ape doctor." He continued, "But I'm getting confused. If Carla turns out to be black, I want to register a protest for her kissing the white Dr. Craig." Despite comments like this, the overall response was positive, and this encouraged me to delve into another social issue: the growing number of young drug addicts.

The widower Jim Craig was a single father raising a daughter. Cathy Craig, a teenager, was very vocal about his not marrying his patient Anna Wolek. But one day when he witnessed her venomous denouncement of Anna, he knew there was something more to her bizarre behavior. When a pharmacist called him about a prescription brought in by a young woman, he recognized Cathy's handwriting. He confided in Anna, who asked Ed Hall (because of his police work with juvenile addicts) what advice he would give to a drug-addicted child. He suggested seeking out a rehabilitation facility called Odyssey House, which was a real place.

This afforded me and *One Life* a fascinating opportunity. I met with Dr. Judianne Densen-Gerber, head of Odyssey House, who explained that we could tape Cathy's treatment there. Each young recovering addict was told that *One Life* was trying to show other young addicts that recovery was possible. If they agreed to participate, we asked them to tell their stories as honestly as possible, since that would be the best way to reach others struggling with addiction. The audience was told that they were seeing real-life addicts and hearing their stories.

The response was enormous. Many addicts in New York reacted to the message by entering Odyssey House. During a taping session, one young woman resident pronounced, "I would be dead if not for this program."

Counseling programs across the country saw a surge in young people ready to get help breaking their addiction. A *New York Times* reporter commented, "Seems to me you're not doing entertainment; you're doing education."

I responded, "I happen to think that education *is* entertaining. Particularly when one learns how to better one's own life." It's a sentiment that would remain important to me throughout my career.

While I was enjoying my ability to tackle important topics on *One Life to Live,* I soon learned, in a most unusual way, that I needed to keep my success in perspective. When Kiki McCabe told Bob and me that her parents were celebrating their seventy-fifth wedding anniversary in Davenport, Bob and I knew that we would be there. It was a warm, loving evening, with many of the family asking Kiki and me questions about our work with *One Life.* Bob Priester's wife, Marjorie, told us of a psychic she had heard about in Davenport who she thought might be a comic character. Her name was Mrs. Quakenbush. I felt that *One Life* had enough comedy with the Viki/Niki situation, but Marjorie's description of the psychic made me curious enough to make an appointment for Kiki and me.

Mrs. Quakenbush was the epitome of "nondescript," from her gray hair to her freshly ironed gray housedress. When we entered her small living room, she looked at me and said, "I'll take you first, dear." Leading me into her compact kitchen, she indicated I should sit on a chair at the table. She said, "I wanted to take you first to tell you about some people who came in with you."

She then specifically described several people from my childhood, including my grandma Dalton. She even described how Grandma Dalton killed the chickens, and then, without dropping a beat, she said, "There's a young man here with you who says his name is Hank. He's wearing a uniform with a metal eagle pin on his chest. He is very tall, and he is standing right behind you. He says to tell you he is always looking after you."

Then Mrs. Quakenbush asked, "What do you do, dear? I would say you are a teacher, but I see millions of people listening to you." Of course that comment made me wonder if she recognized me from a talk show or fan magazine. But she was so earnest that I couldn't help but believe she truly did not know who I was.

When I told her what I did, she clapped her hands and exclaimed, "Oh, yes, that explains it! But you must be careful, dear. Try to stay humble and grateful; don't get proud or puffed up, because it's all coming to you from an Irish ancestor on the other side."

It would be exciting and romantic to have an ancestor who cared enough to help me across the Great Divide. I pictured a stalwart woman who could neither read nor write, crouching by the warm glow of a peat fire, where she told stories to those gathered. But more than anything, my meeting with Mrs. Quakenbush gave me great comfort because it made me feel as if Hank was watching over me—and seeing my early success.

# Chapter 16

# MAKE 'EM LAUGH, MAKE 'EM CRY, MAKE 'EM WAIT

In the early days of *One Life,* I was so busy getting the show off the ground that it was hard to keep up with how big my family was getting. One evening, I said to Bob, "Emily needs a room of her own. This house is too small."

Bob responded, "So that means a new house."

I agreed, so I called a Realtor friend and told him we were house hunting. I added that my interest in early American history made me partial to old houses. That afternoon, the agent took Kiki McCabe and me to see three houses. The last one I saw, I fell in love with. It was built in 1740 on the old Conestoga Road and served as an inn during the Revolutionary War. Washington and Lafayette had stayed there on their way to Valley Forge.

I told Kiki, "This is it!"

She shook her head and said, "Bob Nixon will never buy this."

"Why not?" I asked.

"He will think it needs too many repairs."

"When we needed a new house after Bobby was born, Bob bought our Havertown house without my seeing it, and I didn't like it," I reminded her. "Now it's my turn."

"Are you going to say that to him?" Kiki asked.

"I hope I can find a better way to convince him."

Next door to my 1740 house was the second house we visited. It was a brand-new model home for a subdivision. The builder called it "today's modern home for today's modern young family."

I hated it.

As soon as Bob came home, I started my plan.

"I found our house, honey. You have to come see it now."

"Does it have enough rooms?"

"Absolutely."

On Saturday morning, we pulled up to the sample home and Bob said, "Not much yard."

"We don't need it," I replied. "Just come inside."

As Bob walked in, his face creased in dismay. He said, "Ag, you must be out of your mind. Do you really like this house?"

"Don't you, honey? What's wrong with it?"

"First of all, it doesn't fit the furniture we have, and it doesn't fit our love of early American atmosphere."

I said, "Bob, I see what you're saying; it's not for us. The agent did say the big white house over there is for sale, but it might need a lot of work."

Bob said, "Well, it won't hurt to look."

As we turned in the next driveway, Bob said, "I like the plantings, and this is a real yard. How big is it?"

Trying hard to repress a smile, I said, "Four and a half acres." As we entered the double living room, Bob began to smile.

"This is beautiful. Show me the rest."

As we continued to explore, we found the children's bedrooms, enough closet space for everyone, and a kitchen large enough for a family to live in. Next, he found a proper place for his golf equipment. And for me, under an old slanted roof, there was a perfect room for my writing studio on the third floor. Bob obviously loved the house, but there was only one thing left on his mind.

"The price must be pretty high. How much is it?"

"It's a thousand dollars less than the modern house next door."

He put his arm around me and said, "I think we're home."

AFTER A YEAR, *One Life*'s ratings were consistently good, which meant the network and its affiliates were able to charge advertisers profitable rates. And in television, success leads to a desire for more of the same. Still, I was surprised when ABC's president, Fred Pierce, asked me if I would create another soap opera for them. Although I was no longer writing for *Guiding Light* or *Another World,* I knew the amount of creative work that such a project would entail, and I still had to keep *One Life* successful. Worse yet, there were no new characters in my brain, waiting for me to plot stories for them. I complained to my husband when he came home that evening.

"I just don't have a new show in me right now," I added.

Calm and forthright as always, Bob said, "What about *All My Children*?"

The idea had never crossed my mind. "Do you really think it's good?" I asked.

"I think it's terrific," he said. "I always have, but you weren't hearing me. I guess you were still listening to Harry."

As I stood by our bedroom fireplace with painful memories from the past washing over me, I finally saw that, despite my thinking I was free to be myself, my self-confidence had still not recovered from my father's criticism. It was an oddly liberating realization. I kissed my husband, walked to my desk, and from the bottom drawer removed a package that had lain there, gathering dust, for four years. I boxed it up and sent it to ABC's director of daytime.

His first comment was, "Boy, that was fast work."

The executives read and optioned *All My Children,* setting the premiere for January 5, 1970.

Bob said, "Congratulations, honey! Eat your heart out, CBS!"

To my great joy, my make-believe world was coming to life. Soon the town of Pine Valley would exist, populated by the individuals and families who had lived only in my imagination all these years. By this point, they were so real to me. They clamored to walk the streets, to live their lives and have their stories told. As only my family and a handful of ABC executives have ever read the *AMC* bible, I'd like to share the first few pages.

## ALL MY CHILDREN

### A PROPOSAL FOR A NIGHTTIME OR DAYTIME DRAMA

#### AGNES NIXON, 1965

It means something very special to be a part of this age . . . We are a new breed, spawned by the demands and pressures, the conflicts and longings of a new era . . . Some say we are better than other generations, some say that we are worse, but certain it is that we are different—as different as is our time onstage.

Living in a universe that is constantly expanding while the world is ever shrinking, man is torn between the outer race with progress and the inner search for personal identity—the compulsion to succeed and the need for security . . .

And yet at the center of this conflict, in the core of our being, beyond the loves, hates, and hostilities, our common bond of mankind links us all. This, then, is the underlying theme of All My Children. Not that the concept will be preached in scripts nor that the characters portrayed will necessarily espouse it; quite the contrary, in many cases their fight against this immutability will generate much of the drama.

But underlying our story, the inexorable fact is always there: that in this, our human predicament, what happens to the least affects the great, that the strong are indebted to the weak, that sorrow and fear are the absence of joy and hope, and that without tragedy, there could never be triumph . . .

## STORY OUTLINE

The community of Pine Valley is almost as important a factor in our story as are the characters themselves. A settlement whose roots go deep into pre-Revolutionary soil, the Valley has a distinctive personality and charm, which affects all who live in or near it. And, though it is a self-contained community, its role of suburb to a large, eastern city, as well as its proximity to New York, make it different than most small towns or suburbs in other sections of the country.

Pine Valley has a very fine community-supported hospital, an excellent fire department and police force, one high school, three elementary schools, and a healthy variety of churches, synagogues, and meeting houses.

Although there will be other characters, major and minor, our story, plots, and subplots will deal primarily with three families in Pine Valley: the Craigs, the Tylers, and the Martins . . . Not all members of these families live in Pine Valley, nor will the stories concerning them always take place there, for we shall not be confined to one locale. Yet the "Valley" will be what everyone thinks of when they think of "home." It's home because, whether living there or not, this verdant Valley has, in some way, made them who they are and is, to some extent, a part of them.

Creatively, the new incarnation of *All My Children* was humbling. I had always considered my work ethic my strong suit—hour after hour, day after day, the seat of my pants glued to my chair—but the amount of effort that would be required to write two shows was simply terrifying. I was still responsible for my other make-believe community of Llanview. Could I really do justice to all the residents of Pine Valley?

Even my subconscious was dealing with the fates of my characters. I often awoke with a pressing story idea. Rather than turn on the light and write it down immediately, I would throw a random book from my nightstand on the floor to remind me. In the morning on a scratch pad I recorded my nighttime thoughts. Sometimes Bob counted the books on the floor. "One, two, three, four, five, six. Good ideas?"

I said, "Six nightmares. There is so much to do. I'm afraid I'll screw up. It's going to be a catastrophe!"

Bob pointed to the children in a picture on the wall. "You can stop worrying about your biggest production . . . those four kids. They're turning out pretty damn good, and so will your shows. Anyway, you don't have time to worry about it. Better get dressed and get to work."

So I got up and got to work.

I've often thought the biggest element of successful writing is the ability to get the seat of your pants to the seat of a chair.

The week after the call from ABC, I had to go to New York overnight for meetings with the producers of *One Life,* and also to meet about casting and the countless details involved in the launching of a new serial. I hated being away from the children overnight, but there was just too much for one day. The trip meant taking the local train from suburban Philadelphia to Thirtieth Street Station. From there, I took another train to Penn Station and lugged my suitcase up the stairs to Eighth Avenue to hail a taxi to the Lombardy Hotel. I planned to drop my suitcase there and then catch another taxi to the studio.

As I schlepped my suitcase up the stairs, the enormity of the task sank in. I said to myself, "I'm not going to be of much help to anybody if I have a heart attack on these steps."

When I reached ABC, I explained my fears about my monthly commute to the executives, dragging my suitcase and briefcase from taxi to train, to train, to taxi. Gathering my nerve, I managed to ask them if I could be picked up and driven from my house to the city and back. They readily agreed. I suspect they realized the train was costing them quite a lot of my writing time.

To supply scripts for a daily serial is manifestly impossible for one writer. I had a wonderful *One Life* team with Gordon Russell as my co–head writer, five outline writers, and five scriptwriters. I was responsible for writing the long-term story, a broad projection of about fifty pages in which I detailed the year's seminal events. However, since we were all immersed in the characters and daily life in Llanview, the writers were welcome to offer changes in plot trajectory. Gordon and I were always receptive to the writers' ideas, but always on guard against a change that would damage the symbiosis of the carefully interwoven plotlines. At times, I felt like I was a watchdog protecting the honesty of the plotlines. Don't misunderstand. I was not only protecting the validity of the story line from variations from others on my team; I was also guarding against ideas that would jump into my own mind.

So I was always running a mental review. I ran through story lines while pushing the grocery cart, driving to a parent-teacher meeting—even, I must admit, during church services. I was constantly thinking of my characters and how they blended into the overall story. I was always alert to everyday circumstances, because ideas could come to me from everywhere. I was still wrestling with the proper name for Joe Martin's daughter when I attended the May Fair at my children's school. Walking to the parking lot I overheard a mother calling to her little girl, "Tara, I'm here." Immediately I knew that Tara Martin would soon begin her life in Pine Valley.

While I was playing watchdog with my *One Life* writing team, I had the opposite problem to worry about with *All My Children;* there, I was starting from scratch. As the show was gearing up for production, I still needed to assemble my team. Fast. I was looking for three outline writers and four dialogists. Over the years, I had become acquainted with many writers and was always on the lookout for creative assistance. Many people came to me by recommendation. Others came my way in more unusual circumstances. One hire originated with a high school student who was determined to join our writing team. His work wasn't accepted, and he went off to college. But at school, he told everyone, including the dean of freshmen, that he had written for *All My Children.* A few days later, I received a letter from Lorraine Broderick, dean of new students at the college. Lorraine's letter said, "I told myself that if this young man can write for *All My Children,* then so can I. I love *All My Children,* and would love a chance to be associated with it."

Intrigued, I telephoned Lorraine and asked her to come have dinner with me. She did, and I ended up hiring her to write a sample script. She took a few days off from her job at the university and joined us at the roundtable, where her talent became very obvious. Lorraine was hired to create outlines, and since that day, she has been a very successful soap opera writer. She said that she was grateful for having the job as dean because it brought her to *All My Children.* And I was grateful for the young student's braggadocio because, through him, we acquired a wonderful talent.

In most cases, I gave a promising writer a trial outline or

script before deciding who should be signed to the team. We needed to produce five ready-for-production scripts a week, fifty-two weeks a year. Sitcoms like *All in the Family* aired just once a week and then went into reruns during the summer. But just as the real world never stops, neither did my make-believe world, because soaps never go on hiatus.

When *All My Children* launched, I wrote each outline, which was usually ten to fifteen pages long, and then sent it to one of my four scriptwriters about five weeks before the episode's airdate. He or she would return a thirty-five-to-forty-page draft for me to edit. (Later, one of the talented outliners I hired would take over this responsibility.) Then the dialogist had one week to work on the script and send it to the writers' office. Finally, I read and approved it, and forwarded it to the production team and network. In reading and approving a script, I looked for it to adhere to the initial projection and for the characters to develop organically. It was all very confusing and worrisome, because it seemed like I was doing everything myself—all from my third-floor aerie. And of course I had to do it all over again for *One Life to Live*.

In all that chaos, I realized I needed a comrade in arms, a trusted, kindred writing spirit who could step in for me when necessary, since my children occasionally got sick (and so did I). With so many people depending on me as head writer, I knew it would be irresponsible to pretend that balancing work and family life would always be easy.

I remember the time my nine-year-old son came into my studio to do his homework. When I saw he wasn't getting much written, I went over and touched his shoulder. "Get to work, buddy." To my dismay, he let out a pained scream, and when Bob came home, we took him to the children's hospital. His undiagnosed condition confused the staff, and I moved into a Philadelphia hotel while he was tested. I took my Dicta-phone with me to the hotel so that I could work between hos-pital visits.

At grand rounds, the doctors were fascinated by my son's definition-defying medical case. A doctor from England even-tually diagnosed Bobby with viral radiculitis, an infection of the nerve ganglia mostly found in men who had been in combat. He was cured, and we brought him home. However, the antibiotic he received weakened his immune system, and he came down with acute pneumonia. When I took his temperature, it was 105, and the doctor advised me to bring him back to the hospital. Driving home from the hospital, Bobby had looked over at me and said, "Momma, please don't ever let me go back to that hos-pital." And I promised him he would not. So I told the doctor, "I want to nurse him at home." It was a rough ordeal, but Bobby survived, and we all recovered from the shock.

Given the unpredictability of raising children, it was by happy chance that I found the very talented Wisner Washam to partner with me as assistant head writer to lead this congenial group on *All My Children*. His beautiful wife, Judith Barcroft, whom I had the pleasure of writing for on *Another World,* had introduced us. For some time, Wisner had been employed by Mike Nichols in all phases of his theatrical productions. He sent me a sample *Children* script, and I saw the possibilities.

I realized he would be an ideal second in command because of his eye for drama in everyday life. I told him what I had in mind and what his position would entail. He would work closely with me on the execution of the long-term story, and he would also read all the outlines and scripts as they came in, handling any minor disagreements that might arise with production. In my absence, he would have the authority to make any decisions in my name. Wisner was very interested in giving it a try. This meant he had to learn not just how to out-line, but how to think as I did. I appreciated that he was taking on a very different kind of work as his livelihood.

The basic *All My Children* story began with my long-term projection that encompassed a year, and the network loved it. Further suggestions and changes to the plotlines could be made by anyone on the writing team when we gathered in the large conference room at what became known as "the roundtable." While I alone made the final call on changes in the plot, these roundtable meetings were very frank, with no opinions with-held. It is for this reason that I say we were a team. Though not a word-for-word reenactment, the following may give an idea of how we'd work through a plotline—in this case, how Nick Davis would find out Philip was his biological son—at the roundtable:

AGNES: Nick would love to know Philip is his son. Would Amy tell him?

WISNER: No, it would destroy her marriage.

AGNES: How about this: we have Erica learn it by accident and tell Philip.

JACK: Do you think she would go that far?

AGNES: What do you think?

JACK: I think Erica is focused on what terrible thing she can do next. That's the amazing thing about Erica as a character; she will stop at nothing.

AGNES: Could we have Erica in the previous episode tell Philip that Ruth is not his mother, she is his aunt, and Amy is his mother? Then he runs into Chuck Tyler.

WISNER: Erica thought Phoebe Tyler looked down upon her, so she would go and tell Phoebe.

JACK: I don't know if Erica would do such a terrible thing. She would see how her dirty deed would play out.

AGNES: I think you're right. And it will give the audience time to see what Erica hath wrought.

My storytelling philosophy at these sessions could best be described as "Make 'em laugh, make 'em cry, make 'em wait." Several people have credited me with that maxim, but the concept was used long ago in vaudeville to keep the audience coming back.

Making audiences laugh and cry was almost second nature to me, and an example of making them wait was when we had Nick Davis return to Pine Valley. His reappearance could have been a bombshell because the audience was eager to see how Ruth, Amy, and Ted Brent would feel when they found out Nick was in town. Would Philip learn the truth of his conception and birth? We made that revelation almost happen several times, which served to whet the audience's appetite for it. That's the essence of "making them wait."

Living up to my "Make 'em laugh, make 'em cry, make 'em wait" maxim on a regular basis wasn't always easy, but we usually succeeded because of our well-oiled process from script to air. Every once in a while, however, something unpredictable called for extra effort from the writing team. Any time the network execs planned to preempt an established program, they gave us ample advance notice. This occurred three weeks before Christmas of 1978, when they told us that *AMC* would be replaced with a special on December 24. This allowed us to plot for the week of December 21–25, knowing that we only had to write four shows for that week.

However, on December 17 I received a letter from ABC's director of daytime programming saying a mistake had been made. They would *not* be preempting December 24, and we should supply them with a show. (*Thanks a lot!* I remember thinking.) The entire week of four outlines had already been sent out. Everyone turned to me and said, "What are we going to do?" Taking a deep breath, I replied, "I guess I'm going to write the script."

I dreaded the rush job—especially with all the gift-wrapping I'd put off, and the tree trimming and Christmas decorating that I was determined to do with my kids—but finally I decided to make it a purely Christmas Eve–themed episode for the *All My Children* characters, so that each could find the true meaning of the Christmas spirit.

I received many compliments about the script, but the best one was from the young woman who normally would have had to write that episode. She told me she was reading the script lying in bed with her husband. When she got to the end of it, she tossed it aside, exclaiming, "I give up. It's beyond me!"

Besides hiring a great writing team, the other key part of creating a successful show is finding the perfect actors to inhabit the roles you write—and the gods of casting were astonishingly helpful to us with *AMC*. Without exception, the actors we cast were in every way superb. Besides their remarkable talents, their personalities were so kind and giving that we formed a family of our own almost immediately. That spirit of sharing and empathetic warmth carried through the cameras and television sets to reach our wonderful audience. One of the reasons *Children* was so popular was because our actors truly cared about each other.

For example, the wonderful actor Ray MacDonnell portrayed Joe Martin. He radiated a goodness that made the audience love him. When I saw him in *The Edge of Night,* he reminded me of my own husband. I, too, loved him and wanted him for Dr. Joe.

We also made a great coup by casting Broadway actor Hugh Franklin as Dr. Charles Tyler, Ruth Warrick as Phoebe Tyler, Julia Barr as Brooke English, and David Canary in the double role of the twin Chandler brothers. Karen Gorney was an ideal Tara, and Richard Hatch's portrayal of Philip Brent captured the hearts of many young American women. I did not anticipate the power of their on-screen chemistry. Their young love was so electric that the audience clamored for them to be together, and it infused my storytelling for many years to come.

And now about Erica. Finding the right actor to play this complex high school senior was one of our biggest casting challenges. As my creative juices began to flow, I knew I would have a male doctor with a daughter and a son who would return to Pine Valley. His daughter would be a lovely young teenager named Tara. Both Philip and his best friend, Chuck Tyler, would fall in love with her. But there had to be another young woman in the cast—or so I thought.

However, I was reluctant to have another nice, lovely girl like Tara. Along with *Guiding Light,* I had dialogued on *As the World Turns,* and on that show, Irna had used two characters named Penny and Ellen, who were best friends. They were very nice and nothing like Erica, and they had some wonderful story developments and plot twists. But I didn't want to mimic Irna on my show. So I asked myself, "What do I want? A bad girl?"

Maybe, yes. But I didn't want the audience to dislike her; she had to be popular. But what was the essence of that girl?

Earlier I mentioned that the comic strip character Tillie the Toiler may have inspired the beginnings of Erica's persona. Another source of inspiration was my feelings about Grandma Dalton. Often, when she accused me of being spoiled or told me that children should be seen and not heard, or that I had no respect for my elders, I felt angry and wished I could tell her a thing or two. But at such a young age, playing with my paper dolls, I didn't have the temerity or vocabulary to speak up.

As a teenager, my desire to challenge my grandmother was just as strong. Because of her age and my respect for Mother and Aunt Emma, I restrained myself. But I still recalled the turbulent emotions she aroused. Now I needed a teenage character who could vent all that long-dormant, pent-up emotion. She would need a reason for having such an attitude toward her mother. But first, what was her father's name? In my head, something whispered, "Eric." Then, in my mind, it all fell into place. Early on, when Erica was nine, Eric Kane left his wife and daughter to become a famous movie director in Hollywood, promising to send for them. But he never did. This abandonment gnawed at Erica's self-confidence for the rest of her life.

So Erica began to develop into the human being she became, someone who was determined to wreck any girl's romance with any good-looking boy.

Erica's psychological drama stemmed from the resentment she felt toward her mother, whom she blamed for her father's rejection. She had it out for other women because she thought that they were equally incapable of keeping a man. Therefore, any boy who paid attention to another girl was fair game for Erica. To break up a young romance by winning the boy was, in her subconscious, equivalent to getting her father back, and, in the process, punishing her mother. Of course, when Erica

accomplished this, she soon lost interest in the paternal replace-
ment, and the drama would start all over again as she looked
for her next conquest.

Increasingly, as I created Erica, it dawned on me that much
of her inner suffering was connected to my relationship with
my father. I think that, for a young person, a schism between
parents has a profound effect. It certainly did for me. I saw how
much a father meant to my friends who had theirs, and because
my father rejected me, I always felt inferior to them. Although
my mother left my father, he abandoned me by refusing to support me emotionally, and then he abandoned my whole family
by refusing to communicate, visit, or respond to my letters.

I was busy churning out scripts bringing Erica Kane to
life—particularly through her machinations to steal Philip
Brent from Tara Martin—but I was also panic-stricken because
we still had no one to play her. Our casting director searched
the entire country, and still no one seemed right. That is, until
the producer, Bud Kloss, called me. "I think we've found her.
She was on her honeymoon. Wait until you see the tape."

A videocassette was driven down to Pine Cottage, and as
soon as I saw it, I knew Bud was right. Susan Lucci gave us a
determined seventeen-year-old who knew what she wanted in
life and didn't care whom she might hurt to get it. Of course
Erica had psychological baggage, and her mother, Mona,
played so well by Frances Heflin, often defended her to friends
by saying, "But Erica suffers so." But Susan's performance always helped the audience understand this and, therefore, forgive Erica Kane's heinous acts.

Susan told me that the first time we met, she was surprised
by how friendly I was. But Susan's surprise can't compare to
mine on seeing her audition tape. Although I'd tried to conjure

up a visual image of Erica Kane, all attempts had failed. As soon as I saw the tape I knew why: Susan Lucci *was* Erica Kane. It wasn't just her beauty; it was her ability to transmit to the screen the essence of the character and her subtle interpretation of the role. As I watched her play Erica, story ideas started popping into my head, especially in terms of her disregard for other girls' feelings.

What if she could get Philip to tutor her in geometry? What if I could show her manipulating her mother to get that plain-Jane Tara out of Philip's head?

Susan is my idea of the consummate actress. She not only correctly interprets the meaning of a scene, but time and time again, I have seen her find a nuance in a line of dialogue that I myself didn't realize was there. That interpretation of that line could suggest a new plot point or twist that helped in my story development.

For instance, in an early scene, Chuck asked why Erica wanted to go to California.

Her answer was, "Well, Pine Valley is not the corner of Hollywood and Vine."

The way she delivered that line made us see that this high school senior would stop at nothing to get her way. Right then and there, I decided to make her aspire to be a model. It started a terrific plotline.

Susan and I have enjoyed a long and close friendship, bringing richness to both our professional and private lives. We often joyfully marvel about our blessed collaboration that has captivated audiences for 10,920 episodes across forty-two years. I have often said that although Erica Kane emerged as the paper doll Tillie the Toiler before evolving to the new girl at Pine Valley High, Susan brought so much to the role that I bow to her as cocreator. Susan often says she never tired of playing Erica. I never tired of writing for her, and her legion of fans never tired of watching.

One of the final casting steps came when ABC decided to air *All My Children* and the head of daytime said we had to get a big Hollywood name to make viewers tune in. I disagreed. I told him, "The best star for a daytime serial is a daytime serial star beloved by the audience."

Such a star was Rosemary Prinz, who played Penny, a very popular character on CBS's *As the World Turns*. Rosemary had left that show ten months earlier because her contract was up and she wanted to explore nighttime opportunities. Her fans wrote many letters and were very vocal about how they missed her. I sent her a telegram asking her to have dinner with me. During our meal, I told her that my new show was going to ABC and that I would love to have her as the star attraction. Rosemary said to me, "Agnes, my life is devoted to fighting the war in Southeast Asia. I will be in your series if you promise me that my character will be violently opposed to the war in Vietnam."

I told her that was just what I intended, knowing her political stance and that the network had assured me that it could be an important factor in the show. She said, "If you can personally guarantee that, and that my character can organize marches and partake in rallies on the air, I will do the show."

During dinner, I let Rosemary know I understood war was a gross tragedy that robbed young men of their lives and young women of their loves, and devastated families. I told Rosemary that, in 1941, my fiancé Hank and I went to war protests in Davenport with his parents. I told her about listening to President Roosevelt break the news about Pearl Harbor on that night that changed our lives. Seeing that my words were from my heart, Rosemary said, "Bless you, Agnes. Nothing can stop me from being on your show."

The only promo leading up to *AMC*'s debut was Rosemary standing in front of the camera saying, "Hello, my name is Rosemary Prinz. I'm coming back to television on a serial on ABC entitled *All My Children,* starting January 5. I hope you'll join me."

The national division over the Vietnam War in 1970 was reflected in the opposing opinions of Amy and her in-laws, Dr. Charles Tyler and the hawkish Phoebe, who voiced the suspicion that her antiwar-activist daughter-in-law might be a Communist. Amy's opposition to the war was fueled by the fact that Philip was a high school senior who could soon be drafted. The intense family conflict over Vietnam was a continuous story that we hoped would allow our audience to feel their point of view.

My desire was to show what I knew all too well: the pain of a young woman who had lost her love at war. I wanted our writing team to present these opposing viewpoints honestly, allowing us to humanize the ideology. Our fans were so affected by this story that it began heated conversations in similarly divided families across the country. Much press attention was given to our political story line. For me, it was always personal.

As I wrote the story of Phil being drafted into the air corps, I couldn't help but think of my years with Hank. Planning to marry secretly on the eve of his departure, Phil and Tara were trapped in a blizzard but found an unlocked church and married themselves. Phil shipped out and was soon reported MIA. Then, as soap operas tend to go, later he was found alive.

Writing Phil and Tara's love story was so close to my heart that it brought back tender memories, which of course were followed by such heartache. The scene of Philip's return was emotional for me because of the love Tara had for him, and because it was the ending I had prayed for when Hank was MIA. But if I couldn't control the real world, at least in my make-believe world, I could have the hero return home to the woman who loved him more than anything.

# Chapter 17

# THE POWER OF THE PENCIL

The positive reaction and strong ratings for the Vietnam War story were heartening. But it was the responses from viewers across the country saying that it had caused them to examine their positions that made me want to tackle even more important topics.

One plotline featured Anne Tyler, as played by Judith Barcroft, in a tragic child abuse story we were doing on *AMC*. In preparation, I interviewed Dr. Vincent Fontana, who had detailed this occurrence in his book *Somewhere a Child Is Crying*. What I learned from Dr. Fontana, and had my character Anne Tyler learn, is that most people think child abuse occurs among low-income families. However, it is just as prevalent among well-to-do parents. They just happen to have the money to "hospital shop" and can afford to take their battered children to facilities where they will not arouse suspicion.

In our telling of this story, Anne had a well-to-do friend who was able to hide her abusive treatment of her little girl. In the drama, Anne was able to make her friend accept the fact that she had a problem and was hurting the child she loved. I found a group in Philadelphia called Child and Parental Emergency (CAPE) that helped needy parents face the problems they were trying to hide. Anne Tyler became very active in CAPE. Further research revealed that many cities had organizations like

CAPE, and the network was able to persuade stations to run a banner encouraging anyone who needed help to call the number on-screen after the episode. It also said their anonymity would be respected. The president of the Philadelphia CAPE group told me they were swamped with calls from parents who needed help, and one mother joined the group and specifically devoted her time to reach out to help low-income parents.

Sometimes writing about one social issue led to another. From the beginning, I knew I wanted Philip to be discovered alive after going MIA but never gave much thought to how his return would play out. Then in one of the endless dreams in which my characters appeared, I saw Philip hanging on an airplane wing, floating down a river, and a Vietnamese child swimming to the rescue.

In the morning, I knew I had my rescue scene. As I wondered who could play that child, I thought of Binh Scott, the adopted ninth child of our dear friends Sandra and Dick Scott. Although they had eight children, the plight of the Vietnam War orphans had moved them to action. Dick was a good golfing buddy of Bob's, and he and Sandra shared the details of their trip to Vietnam and the orphanage where they'd found Binh. The boy was ten years old and a double amputee who had lost his legs after being run over by a US Army truck. I remembered seeing Binh at Aronimink Golf Club diving expertly off the diving board as everyone congratulated him.

Bob and I asked Dick and Sandra about Binh's being on the show, and they agreed to let us ask him. He gave us an enthusiastic yes. For our first location shoot, we dressed a small section of the Connecticut River as the Mekong. On a Friday afternoon, Ruth was putting away some of Philip's things, and the scene cut to a plane wing floating down the Mekong River. There was someone clinging to the wreckage. Then viewers saw Binh Scott swim to the wing, pull Philip off, and swim with him toward shore. When he managed to get Philip to the riverbank, Binh pulled himself up using only his arms. It was then that the audience realized that this was because he had no legs.

No television show had ever cast an amputee. We were amazed by the many letters we received from others with similar disabilities, thanking us for giving them the courage not to be embarrassed by lost limbs. A very nice postscript occurred later. One Sunday afternoon, Binh called me. "Mrs. Nixon," he said, "I would like to come over and show you how I have grown." His father brought him over to show off his new prosthetic legs. Binh went on to graduate from college. He went back to Vietnam to connect with his roots and met his wife. Married with children, he now runs a successful business there.

Because there was so much controversy after the US Supreme Court's *Roe v. Wade* decision in 1973, I also wanted to bring that real-world topic into my Pine Valley world. So I came up with the following plot: Erica Kane's pregnancy threatened her plans for a modeling career, so she decided to have an abortion. Without telling her husband—but telling the hospital that he knew about it and approved—she went through with the procedure. Over lunch, I told Brandon Stoddard, the head of ABC Daytime, my idea of Erica having an abortion, and he thought it was a terrific and topical story and that it was going to get big ratings. He gave the story projection, which I had written, to Standards and Practices. To my relief, they did not object to its production or request any script changes.

The audience's reaction to the story, however, was divided. The right-to-life faction was opposed on general principles. Surprisingly, the pro-choice group criticized us for having the wrong person have the abortion; Erica was not a "good" enough character. The kind of woman needed to promote the pro-choice option was the admirable and unimpeachable Nurse Ruth.

My own view on legalizing abortion was that since so many illegal abortions were being performed, the restrictions on the procedure were a farce, and they were putting women's lives in danger. Surprisingly, not many of my fellow Catholics criticized me for airing the abortion subject. My husband, who was a convert to Catholicism, was also pro-choice.

The many letters from the pro-choice and pro-life camps made me glad that people were interested enough in the show to write. I didn't mind the criticism; it meant that our show was helping people voice their opinions. The intensity of the audience's feelings about the show was an amazing and gratifying phenomenon to me. The praise and love from people who sought me out was mind-boggling.

In 1974, in the wake of these important plotlines, we were nominated for an Emmy for best writing team, but we did not win. Leaving the theater without trophies and feeling a bit down, I heard a big commotion. Growing worried, I asked my son, "What's wrong? Why is everyone running down the street?"

Bobby said, "Nothing's wrong. It's a few of your fans. They're shouting, 'We love you, Aggie!'"

It was so encouraging to hear them saying how important the show was in their lives and to keep up the good work.

Sometimes the issues I addressed on my shows hit closer to home. One emerged from a conversation I had with my friend Babs as we shopped for a dress for one of my talk show appearances. Babs was one of the few women who felt I could be a good mother *and* keep a writing career. We were so close that we could discuss my constant worry that my kids were growing up so fast, and I was missing it because of *All My Children*.

"You're different from other women; your mind gets things done faster," she told me. "Stop knocking yourself down."

"The problem is, I'm not as fast as my children."

"What are you talking about?"

"You know how I like to work out in the sun behind the garage with the telephone to keep in touch with production?"

"Yes?"

"Well, last week while I was sitting there, I saw one of Bobby's school friends come past me and head to the fields where Sadie grows her vegetables. 'Hello, Jimmy,' I said, but when he saw me, he took off like a jackrabbit. Curiosity got the better of me, so I called Bob at work and told him what happened. 'What do you suppose is special about that field?' I asked.

"He answered, 'I'm going to find out.'

"When Bob questioned Bobby about the incident, he replied, 'I'm growing marigolds for your table, Mom.' Bob looked at me and said, 'Marigolds, hell. It's marijuana.' Turning to Bobby, he said, 'Don't you know you put your mother's life in jeopardy! One of your drug-crazed friends could have killed her to get to the pot.'"

"So what did he do to Bobby?" Babs asked.

"Bob was so mad, he set the field on fire. Then he took Bobby in the car and turned him in to his friend the police chief, who said, 'You did the right thing turning Bobby in, but I can't arrest him because you burned the evidence.'"

After I finished the story, Babs asked, "You don't think that was your fault, do you?"

"No, not exactly my fault. But perhaps I should be more aware of what they're doing with their time."

"I'm glad they didn't lock Bobby up," Babs said. "Remember what that minister said when he spoke to us about the prevalence of teenage drugs and alcohol?"

I said, "Oh, yes. I asked him where the young people get drugs and alcohol."

Babs said, "And remember his answer?"

I said, "He looked straight at us and said, 'Parents, your children get alcohol from all of your houses. That's where it starts.'"

The next day, after I got the kids off to school, I was back at my outdoor writing chair—the "scene of the crime"—ready to begin my morning writing stretch from eight a.m. until one p.m., when I would go in for lunch and watch the show. I hoped to get four outlines written, but I couldn't avoid feeling guilty about Bobby. And then it hit me: I was doing the best that I could. I was being productive while the kids were in school for most of the day. And I was a good example for my daughters of a mom who was fulfilled by doing work that she loved. Sitting there, I realized that I wasn't a bad mother at all. In fact, because I loved doing my job, it made me a *better* mother.

And even if we had some skirmishes at home, at least my kids weren't running away. On Sunday, November 17, 1975, the *New York Times Magazine* ran an article by Ted Morgan titled "Little Ladies of the Night." The subtitle read, "Today's runaway is no Norman Rockwell tyke. Instead, she may well be a 14-year-old in hot pants on New York's Minnesota Strip." Morgan reported that hundreds of runaway girls from the Midwest came to New York City and were quickly lured into teenage prostitution. Pimps were a constant at the Port Authority Bus Terminal, just waiting to add to their roster.

The article stressed the horror these young girls faced at

home before running away, but the life that awaited them in New York was far worse. I was very moved by the piece, and eight weeks after it appeared, *All My Children* began the story of Donna Beck and Tyrone, the pimp who recruited Donna minutes after she stepped off a bus from Minnesota. In Tyrone's hands, she was virtually a slave. He abused her sexually and beat her when she did not make the quota of daily tricks he demanded.

One night, Tyrone thought he had beaten Donna to death. He drove out of the city and dumped her body on the outskirts of Pine Valley. Dr. Chuck Tyler found her on his way to his residency at the hospital. Donna was still alive, but she had a long convalescence. During this time, she and Chuck developed a deep friendship, which eventually became love. Their story, with a plethora of plot twists—especially when Tyrone was determined to reclaim Donna—captivated our increasingly young audience. But to me, even more heart-rending was what Richard Van Vleet, the actor playing Chuck Tyler, experienced.

Since he lived in New Jersey, Richard took a bus to Manhattan and then walked from the station to the studio on West Sixty-Sixth Street each day. On numerous occasions, young women approached him with the plea, "Dr. Tyler, would you help me get out of the life?"

Two years later, ABC aired a movie of the week entitled *Little Ladies of the Night.* I felt proud of my part in raising awareness of this growing problem.

Occasionally, I was humbled to learn that sometimes I didn't even need story lines to help the viewers of my shows. One day, I was scheduled to appear on Barbara Walters's show *Not for Women Only.* An ABC guard would usually take the show's audience to and from their seats in the studio. But somehow that day, the guard wasn't able to control the viewers, and they slipped away from him. Most headed toward Barbara's other guests. Then one young man said in a loud voice, "Mrs. Nixon, it's imperative that I talk to you." This got my attention, so I stopped and waited for him to reach me.

He said, "Thank you so much for talking to me. When I was in high school, I was such a fan of *All My Children* that I wrote you a letter telling you that I loved your show, that it mattered to me, but that I felt my life didn't matter to anyone and I didn't know what to do. You answered my letter and said that I had to realize that my life was very important to everyone else in the world, that I must finish high school, go to college, and remember the theme we live by: you are all my children. I just want to say thank you. I'm studying English now and have a three point seven GPA."

Given that my work had so often taken time away from my children—who were now twenty, nineteen, eighteen, and fifteen—what the young man said to me made me feel a bit better. I had helped a young unknown boy find his place in the world. I couldn't ask for much more than that.

# Chapter 18

# THE RATINGS SPEAK

By 1975, *All My Children* was something of a phenomenon, and the show was making ABC a great deal of money. Even so, inevitably it wanted to increase its revenue. Fred Pierce, the president of the network, made a big pitch to increase the show to an hour. I resisted because I thought it worked great as a half hour, and I was fearful of how doubling my workload might affect my personal life. Of course, I also worried about *One Life,* because I was already not giving it the same time I'd used to, pre-*AMC.* Between 1970 and September 1973, I was head writer for both shows. Even with my fantastic co–head writers—Gordon Russell on *One Life* and Wisner Washam on *Children*—it was madness. I was working at all times of the day and night. Doing daily chores, I would be thinking about a story for *One Life* and then switch to imagining a plot for *All My Children.* I worried about how I'd manage all the story ideas swirling in my head.

After the first year and its constant demands, I began to feel like I was drowning. Bob saw how I was sinking and insisted I get a secretary to translate the notes I had. Rita Sulger came to work with me at Pine Cottage. Whenever I wrote a piece of dialogue or a script, she became so in tune with the characters that she would know who was speaking.

Because of the time crunch, I could only read two or three

final scripts per week. But it was enough to make sure that everything was on track and that both shows were delivering the drama necessary for generating good ratings. As mentioned earlier, every day when I was home, I went down to the kitchen and ate lunch on a tray in the "playroom" next to the kitchen while I watched the shows. It was my way of making sure the quality didn't slip. Sadie and Joseph often joined me.

It was very convenient because *AMC* aired at one p.m. and *One Life* was at one thirty. I always had a notepad and pencil by my side so I could jot down story ideas that occurred to me. When the show was wonderful, it was the high point of my day, but when it missed the mark, I was very upset. I spent a lot of time pondering what went wrong: Was it the writing, acting, or directing, or something in the long-term story projection? Once I figured out the problem, I was determined to correct the mistake and prevent it from happening again.

I sorted through the many ideas for both shows in my head and made notes on paper. Then I dictated to Rita the long-term story projection for each serial. She typed the formal document to send to the network and to my writing and production teams. If I was in New York, Gordon came to my personal office at the studio each week. We sat down, and he outlined to me his ideas for the forthcoming story development. I either agreed with him, or made suggestions or changes. These meetings could take from ten minutes to an hour.

Bob and I had some serious discussions about whether I could come up with enough stories for *AMC* to fill up an hour each day, five days a week, fifty-two weeks per year. I didn't know if I could handle it. When I tried to dissuade Fred Pierce from expanding *AMC* to an hour, I explained that we would need a bigger studio. He said he would solve that by building a whole new one. At that point, I started creating characters and stories to support the doubled airtime. The network agreed to make Gordon Russell, who had worked beautifully with me on *One Life,* the show's head writer.

So *All My Children* was soon going to be an hour long. Not to be outdone, my children kept me busy as well. Our second-oldest child, nineteen-year-old Mary, stunned us when she announced her engagement to her boyfriend. She added to our shock by saying they wanted to get married the following week, so that she could move in with him when he started fall classes at Georgetown University, as a freshman.

Bob and I were dismayed that Mary was determined to take this life-changing step, and we tried to talk her out of it. But she had made up her mind, and at eighteen, there was little we could do but support her. Despite the shortage of time, we had a lovely service at the beautiful church on the Villanova campus and a reception at Pine Cottage. It was nice, but I felt deprived of long-held plans for elaborate weddings for our daughters. (Perhaps this was played out on-screen with some of the characters' fancy weddings.) Nine months later, we were delighted to become grandparents with the arrival of Ceara, a Gaelic name that means "born with armor."

Meanwhile, Cathy planned to marry a young man she had fallen in love with on a blind date. His name was Paul Chicos, and there was no doubt she wanted to spend the rest of her life with him. As one of her best friends said, "Cathy chased Paul until he caught her." Planning another wedding at Pine Cottage was a busy affair, but I was in my glory because Cathy was so happy. Emily, our family humorist, said, "Mom was so excited when Cathy got married that she had the whole house redecorated from top to bottom. But the reception was outside, so no one even saw it."

With Bobby working at a wildlife preserve, three of the

children were now gone from the house, so we were grateful that Emily, our baby, was still a junior in high school. The many roles she won in the drama department plays made it clear she had talent as an actress, and we delighted in seeing her onstage. Bob and I loved going to her performances, and we always brought Sadie, who cherished Emily as if she were her own daughter.

Around this time Bob and I went to New York for about three days every other week. He eventually sold the Chrysler dealership to become the co–executive producer of both shows with me. As a businessman, he understood financial operations and how to keep costs down. For example, he helped me learn about the "play or pay" contracts all daytime actors signed. If Ray MacDonnell was only seen once as Joe Martin for the five-day broadcast and had a two-day guarantee, he was paid accordingly. When I finished plotting for a week of shows, Bob would ask to see my "squares" (as I called those outlines) to determine whether I had used the actors according to the standard twenty-six-week contract. I soon learned to write stories according to those agreements. I wonder if the shows would still be on the air if the networks had stuck to Bob's efficient philosophy. Other people would ask me if I found it difficult having Bob running the business and me on the creative side. I would always explain that it was a most happy partnership.

On April 25, 1977, *All My Children* aired its first hour-long episode. Getting ready for the expansion took more than a year. Twice as much airtime meant twice the number of associate writers, actors, directors, and production staff, as well as a greatly expanded crew. But the primary responsibility for an enlarged story canvas—as I knew all too well—was mine.

After *All My Children* expanded to an hour, Adam Chandler and Palmer Cortlandt, who had been bitter enemies since their youth, became central characters. Palmer Cortlandt was born Pete Clooney and grew up dirt-poor in Pigeon Hollow, West Virginia. He wooed Lottie Chandler, fathered her son Ross, and abandoned her. But it was Pete who felt alone and abandoned, and he blamed others for his unhappiness. When he left Pigeon Hollow, he changed his name to Palmer Cortlandt and made a fortune in electronics. "Palmer" could now afford to purchase Pine Valley's finest home, Cortlandt Manor, but he could never escape his Pigeon Hollow roots. Adam Chandler, who blamed Palmer for his sister's death, hated him and also moved to Pine Valley, with his twin brother.

Palmer fell in love with Daisy, the housekeeper's daughter. They had a child together, Nina, and for years, Palmer had his daughter believe her mother had died, while she was, in fact, very much alive. He had kicked her out when he discovered she was having an affair.

As Palmer was becoming a wealthy man, Adam was determined to wreak havoc on him. Palmer loathed Adam equally for causing his first business to go bankrupt. The warriors jousting on the fields of Pine Valley took many forms, but usually a woman was involved.

For many months, when Adam was on-screen, there was a mysterious occupant in his mansion. What was thought to be a ghost or an intruder turned out to be Adam's lovable twin brother, Stuart. This gentle soul, so different from his twin, played the part of his brother's Jiminy Cricket, always trying to get Adam to lead a more humane life.

One day in the writing of the Palmer Cortlandt/Daisy plotline, Jack Wood, a terrific director and writer, said, "Remember, Agnes, love can be the opposite of hate." (Jack was a constant reminder of what the show was about.) From this idea we progressed to the story line for Palmer and Daisy, who said she couldn't be married to Palmer because of his jealousy. However, she let him know that she'd enjoy sleeping with him whenever he felt like it.

Palmer was so pathologically possessive that he also went to any extremes to keep Nina from her suitors. But, I wondered, how far would he go? That was the question I had to find the answer to.

While mulling this story problem, at age forty-eight, I had early cataract surgery at the Wilmer Ophthalmological Institute of Johns Hopkins Hospital. It turned out to provide a key to the Palmer story line. I became acquainted with Dr. Arnold Patz, director of Wilmer and renowned for discovering that blindness in premature infants was caused by the excessive amount of oxygen in their preemie cribs.

On a quiet Sunday afternoon, Dr. Patz graciously gave me a tour of the hospital, paying special attention to the advances in arresting diabetic retinopathy, a form of blindness caused by diabetes. He showed me the amazing laser beam equipment that directly attacked the affected areas of a patient's eyes, thereby containing the condition. Dr. Patz added that because the treatment was so new, many people suffering from the degenerative disease did not know about it, even though the institute was trying to spread the word. I knew then that I had my plotline, which might also help people with the disease: a romance between the diabetic Nina and Cliff, who was an intern to Dr. Joe Martin.

Palmer was furious when he saw his daughter falling in love with Cliff Warner. The young people were deliriously happy, and Nina told Palmer that Cliff had proposed and she was going to accept. Under the guise of a concerned father, Palmer lied to Nina and told her that she was going blind from diabetic retinopathy. He said he was sure she didn't want to burden Cliff with a blind wife. Heartbroken, Nina put on a believable front and told Cliff she would not marry him because she didn't really love him. Equally heartbroken, Cliff was easy prey for Sybil Thorne, who was determined to marry him. The lovers separated until Dr. Joe Martin, learning of Palmer's treachery, told Nina of the help awaiting her.

The show went on location to Johns Hopkins in Baltimore, where Nina's treatment was explained and replicated on television. The Wilmer Institute furnished a technical film that was edited to show Nina undergoing laser surgery.

When I asked Dr. Patz if he wanted a doctor to play the part of the surgeon, he laughed and said, "I'm sure you can make an actor a better surgeon than I can make a surgeon an actor." So we cast an actor as "Dr. Stone," who then became so seriously injured in an auto accident involving a drunk driver that he could not perform the operation. Cliff was the only qualified surgeon available, and he stepped in and saved Nina's sight.

Making the public aware of a surgical cure for one type of blindness was a television first, and the story was highly rated, reaching more than five million homes. Even more important to me was Dr. Patz's report of the unprecedented number of patients who came for the sight-saving surgery.

Almost twenty years later, on September 29, 1995, I was presented with a plaque for the diabetic retinopathy story line at a ceremony at Johns Hopkins University School of Medicine on the twenty-fifth anniversary of the Retinal Vascular Center of the Wilmer Ophthalmological Institute. I treasure it to this day, and it is displayed on the wall of the family television room.

While I received real-life gratitude for the story line, the amazing actor and dancer James Mitchell, who played the part of Palmer Cortlandt, didn't enjoy the same reception. When

James and I went out to dinner, people came up to us to say what a terrible person he was for trying to keep his daughter from the love of her life.

As you might guess, many people, including cowriters, have asked me if there were elements of my own father's personality in Palmer. My answer has always been yes, there's a great deal of Harry in Palmer, particularly how he became obsessed with something he desired and intent upon destroying anything he thought was in his way.

I remember my grandmother saying that Harry was selfish and only concerned about making money. Sometimes she said he had a problem or was a fly-by-night who would only hurt my mother in the end. Grandma Kate was right; it turned out that Harry had no means to support my mother. Once, I'd been told that Harry was furious when Mother became pregnant with me, because that meant she'd have to quit her job and lose that source of income. As a child, I'd never thought of my father as being "sick." As an adult, creating Palmer, I simply made him the way I saw Harry: mean.

Of course, thinking about my father was never easy for me. I used my writing to study his destructive behavior, to understand how it had affected my life, and to ensure that I didn't inflict any pain on my own four children. I never really believed I might be like Harry or Palmer, but I sometimes thought long and hard about that while writing Palmer's story.

As it turns out, creating Palmer was cathartic. He could try to keep his daughter for himself by telling her she would soon be blind, but I made sure he was unable to. The heinous things he did to his daughter caused the audience to hate him and enjoy his suffering. And unlike in my childhood with Harry, I was in control in Pine Valley—so Palmer Cortlandt suffered tremendously.

It was particularly therapeutic for me to write the Nina role. Like me, Nina eventually uncovered the lies her father told. Nina's father also sought to prevent her from marrying the man she loved. I wanted to make Palmer do awful things because his actions made me able to forgive Harry, since Palmer was so much worse. Eventually, Nina was able to forgive Palmer when he apologized—but only after she married Cliff in a lavish wedding that Palmer had to pay for. Her father also had to suffer through her mother's affairs with a number of attractive men.

As satisfying as it was to work through my feelings about my father, I had always suspected—and perhaps hoped—that there was a deep-seated motivation for his cruelty. My suspicions were finally confirmed about a year after the show expanded to an hour, when I received one of my frequent calls from the saintly and beloved Hazel. In the four years since Harry died, we had grown very close, and our children treasured her visits. Hazel called to tell me she'd heard something extraordinary from an elderly woman she had met in Chicago.

When she learned Hazel was Harry's widow, she said to Hazel, "I knew your husband when he was a child."

Hazel said, "Were you friends with Harry's mother, Mrs. Eckhardt?"

The old woman snorted. "I should say not. A married woman out at the tavern every night with a different man?"

Suddenly my father was revealed to me. I saw him as a seven-year-old with his face pressed up against the windowpane, pleading, "Mommy, please come home. Where are you?"

I'd known Harry had adored his mother, but she couldn't have cared less about him. His past life was built on lies. Finally, I understood why my father had been so intent on my mother's being the perfect housewife and why he had worked so hard to control me. I saw how his mother's behavior must have motivated his drive to succeed. After all, I remembered well how Harry's absence had shaped my own life.

Through Palmer Cortlandt, I tried to understand how someone like Harry could be overwhelmed by the most minute incident, which escalated into lifelong trauma. Trying to understand my father's personality was one reason why I was compelled to create characters who were born innocent but, through tragic circumstances, were rendered evil. And yet, in a sense, they were also helpless victims. In part, writing about these damaged characters was my way of understanding and healing from my father's anger and neglect.

I might have ended Palmer's story on a healing note, but as Jack Wood used to say, "Soap operas are always in the second act." And it was in the second act, in 2010, that we lost the great actor Jimmy Mitchell. Since no actor could ever replace Jimmy, Palmer Cortlandt had to die as well—but this was all coming before I was ready to say good-bye. I never got to write the come-to-Jesus scene I planned, where Daisy could tell Palmer what an awful husband and father he had been. I also wanted to have Palmer admit she was right and finally tell Nina he was sorry. But sometimes television shows, like real life, don't give you a chance for a neat ending.

I also thought of my mother often, especially when it came to Erica Kane. Even though Erica got what she wanted in life, I eventually decided that even the "bad girl," like Tillie the Toiler (and unlike my mother), should get a chance to fall in love on the show. For Tom and Erica's honeymoon in 1978, we wanted a distant and beautiful location. The choice for daytime TV's first long-distance location shoot was easy. I chose St. Croix because the island meant so much to Bob and me. After spending a few vacations there, we'd fallen in love with it and had bought a small hilltop house with a spectacular view of the Caribbean. We ended each day captivated by the beautiful display of the sun setting over the distant hills.

One scene I wrote had Tom and Erica strolling down the beach (how I loved those beaches!). Walking through the sand, Tom mentions that sand is made from crushed shells. Erica is astounded at his breadth of knowledge, but he replies sweetly that he learned it from the brochure in their hotel room.

Many of our production staff came on this trip, as well as our producer, Bud Kloss; director Jack Coffey; Dick Schoenberg; Susan Lucci of course; and wardrobe, hair, and makeup. Our two head writers, Wisner Washam and Jack Wood, were there too, along with Bob and me. It was especially fun because *All My Children* was a huge hit on St. Croix. It came on at six p.m. there, rather than the usual US time slot. This enabled the viewers to watch the show together at home, before video recording became popular. The Cruzans' fondness for the show was so deep that when the local affiliates wanted to move the news to *AMC*'s six p.m. spot, loyal fans rose up in arms and wrote letters of protest.

The fans were so excited that we were filming that they kept crowding around each scene as it was being shot. The director asked them to please vacate the set. Ultimately, he threw up his hands. Then Susan came out and graciously said, "Please let us shoot the scene, and then I can come visit with all of you afterward."

Everyone apologized and one of the fans said, "We will be waiting for you because you asked us to. We found out how nice you are. We love you so much!"

Behind the scenes, it was a lovefest. We had dinner at the Buccaneer hotel, and the entire cast and crew wound up on the dance floor, joined by a swelling legion of local fans. The line of men waiting to dance with Susan stretched around the dance floor and into the hotel lobby. My dear husband enjoyed the Cruzans' love for *All My Children*. The highlight of the shoot was a wrap party that Bob and I had in our home. I made sure we had cocktails scheduled before dinner, because I wanted to share the sunset and panoramic view.

As the sun sank beyond the horizon, it seemed almost mystical how much I cared about my friends who were there with me. Susan was especially enthusiastic about her stay. "I had such a wonderful time," she said. "People treated me as if I was a star."

Her statement struck me because I realized that she *was* a true star—and so was our show.

In 1985, we won the Emmy award for Outstanding Writing. It was one of the most thrilling moments of my life. I'd long dreamed of receiving such an honor, and I had all the writers join me in accepting the award. In my speech, I said how much it meant to be voted the best writing team. I thanked the academy, and especially the audience for all the letters they had written to me, saying how much they loved the show. We promised to work hard to keep our audience entertained in the weeks and months ahead. "You are all my children," I said. My husband was there to share the joy.

Later, my cousin David called to congratulate me. "Aggie, I'm just glad all those years of playing with those damn paper dolls finally paid off for you," he said.

Buoyed by our success, in 1989, we took on one of our most intense stories on *All My Children*—an AIDS story line involving Stuart, Cindy, and related characters. Cindy contracted AIDS from her husband, a heroin addict. After he died, she and Stuart fell in love. Theirs was a very popular romance. Unlike many TV stories about AIDS, however, I chose the more true-to-life ending with Cindy dying from the illness. The writing team unanimously agreed, and we all looked forward to dramatizing the prejudice against the "gay plague." In one case, a young relative of Stuart's even tried to set fire to Cindy's house to keep Stuart from catching the disease. The medical community applauded us for our realistic portrayal, demonstrating to the viewer the true facts about the illness.

By this point, AIDS was sweeping the world with devastating impact. New York was hit especially hard. Every actor and every crew member had lost friends or loved ones. Some gay members of the cast and crew who worked behind the camera were very vocal in their appreciation for what we were doing. But as the story unfolded, everyone knew no thanks were necessary. We were a company of actors and artists, a family fighting the illness. We were supporting one another. Many viewers wrote to applaud us for bringing the taboo subject to television. My favorite letters were the ones that said they loved the story because we showed gays and lesbians to be just ordinary people with the same emotions, hopes, and fears as everyone else. We showed not the differences, but the similarities, and demonstrated that we were all God's children.

One crew member wrote a very moving letter in which she said how much this story line would have meant to her if she had seen it when she was a teenager struggling with her sexual identity. I found her response, and all the responses from people who'd been touched by my shows, very gratifying.

# Chapter 19

# ACTORS AND ME

When *One Life to Live* and *All My Children* started, I didn't have time to go to the studio, and in fact, I wasn't needed on set that much. I knew my place was in my third-floor room at home, writing shows. But when I tuned in each day, it was a true joy to watch our writing brought to life by our brilliant company of actors. Later in my career, I made the most of any opportunity to visit with the actors who graced our shows, and it gives me great pleasure to remember them.

I think first of David Canary, because everyone on the show considered him the most outstanding talent among us. Practically every year, David received a Daytime Emmy nomination; he won five times for Outstanding Lead Actor in a Drama for his dual portrayals of Stuart and Adam Chandler. He was also the most lovable member of the company. His personality was so genuine, and his lack of self-importance was amazing. In fact, he was shy and retiring. A striking example of his kind manner happened ten years ago when my phone rang. David apologized for interrupting me, but I was always delighted by his calls. His daughter was interested in applying to the School of Communication (formerly the School of Speech) at Northwestern, and he wanted to know if I would talk to her about the school and share anything I thought might be useful.

After we hung up, it struck me. I said to myself, "Nixon,

you're so stupid. What David really wants, but wouldn't ask for, is a letter of recommendation."

I called right back and said, "David, would you like me to write a letter for your daughter for college?" He was so surprised and grateful that I had inferred the motivation of his call. I wrote the letter, and David and Maureen later called with the joyful news that she was accepted.

Another example of perfect talent was Julia Barr, who brought Brooke English to life and who would often end a scene with a comic flair. One of my favorite examples of her skill was a brief scene between Brooke and Phoebe, who chastises Brooke, her niece, for socializing with Adam Chandler, her former husband. After Phoebe asks Brooke to promise her that she won't fraternize with Adam again, Brooke responds with a display of her trademark wit:

"Aunt Phoebe, Adam has been very nice to me since the divorce, and I think you can say I'm an example of following my highly admired Aunt Phoebe."

"Brooke, dear, that's so sweet of you to say, and I do hope people will think of you as a representative of our immensely respected family."

"Thank you. I'll see you at dinner."

Brooke then opens the door and leaves a very pleased Aunt Phoebe, but quickly pokes her head out to address her again. "Aunt Phoebe, I must also tell you: the reason I can't stop seeing Adam is that he really turns me on! And you know how that is, Aunt Phoebe!"

I knew Kay Campbell when she played Effie, Ma Perkins's daughter, on that famous radio serial. After the show moved to New York, we became good friends. I was rather shocked to see her name as one of the actors auditioning for Grandma Kate Martin because she seemed so young to me. However, her audition was so perfect, she got the part, and our friendship continued. Kay jokingly kept bugging me to give her a romance with an elderly gentleman next door, Harlan Tucker. Though the subject was humorous for us, it wasn't uncommon. I spent a lot of time listening to actors who wanted to explain how the show would increase its ratings if I would just increase their characters' story lines.

Sometimes an actor objected to a certain line. For instance, one male actor, who was very masculine, came to me with a script in which he offered to toss the salad for his wife at dinnertime. He said, "I can't say that—it's not masculine. Next thing you know, I'll be offering to scrub the kitchen floor." In another case, a very talented actress, who had successful roles on Broadway but was glad to have the weekly stipend of a serial, played a housekeeper who ran a very tight ship. She came to me with a well-written long-term story in which she, the housekeeper, fell madly in love with the butler, and the two of them eloped. I had to nix the idea as it didn't work with our overall plot.

Another story idea came from the wonderful actress Ruth Warrick, who played socially prominent Phoebe Tyler. Nick Davis was starting a dancing class for the well-to-do of Pine Valley and courted Phoebe to help him get a number of patrons. Nick also happened to be in love with Phoebe's daughter, Ann. Ruth wanted to use that situation for what she said would garner high ratings. When Nick and Ann announced their engagement, Phoebe would discover she was pregnant with Nick's baby. It hadn't occurred to Ruth that Phoebe, at sixty-five, couldn't get pregnant.

Frances "Fra" Heflin, who so personified Mona Kane, was the sister of Van Heflin, a well-respected Hollywood actor best known for the movie *Shane*. Hers was one of the few auditions I didn't participate in, but Doris Quinlan, the executive producer, assured me she was perfect.

Fra and I became friendly because she was such a lovely person. We did not have sufficient dressing rooms for every actor in those lean early days, so she shared one with Susan. For all of Susan's enormous talent, there were a few things she felt that she lacked for a live-on-tape television show. She voiced her concern about this to Fra, who said, "It's very simple, and I will show you." Within a few days, Fra made Susan comfortable and ideal in that format.

A few months later, Fra's son, Jonathan Kaplan, produced a movie. Susan and her husband, Helmut, accompanied Fra and her husband to the premiere at Lincoln Center. After the credits, Fra went to the ladies' room. She went inside a stall as a gaggle of young girls came in. One said, "Did you see Erica was here? Why do you think she came?" Authoritatively Fra said, "Erica came because her mother told her to," and made a stately exit. Over the years, the actors' combination of talent and good humor brought a great deal of happiness to my life.

SOMETIMES MY RELATIONSHIP with the actors bordered on the supernatural, especially when it came to their love lives. In 1981, the characters of Dr. Frank and Nancy Grant took into their home the son of Frank's sister, who had died a year earlier. Jesse had grown up in a tough neighborhood in Center City and still had a few rough spots that the Grants tried to remove. He was a good kid, and as soon as he spotted Angie, he developed a true affection for her. Jesse and Angie became the first black teenage love story on daytime, and they became enormously popular. The audience faithfully followed their story as it built through many vicissitudes and heartrending separations. Judge Watkins, Angie's father, thought Jesse would never outgrow his tough upbringing. Jesse became close friends with Greg and Jenny, who were classmates at Pine Valley High and who made him a part of their clique. They thought that Jesse and Angie had the right to be together, which put them in direct conflict with Judge Watkins. And so the two factions, battling over Jesse and Angie's love, were the basis of a typical Pine Valley romance.

It so happened that the actors playing the very popular couple Dr. Frank and Nancy Grant, John Danelle and Lisa Wilkinson, were married in real life. One day in the studio I joined John and Lisa for lunch and they shared that they were thinking of adopting one of the many infants who needed and deserved a home.

I said to them, "Well, you're going to have a baby on the show."

Three months later, my phone rang, and it was Lisa. "Agnes, I'm pregnant." In a very serious voice, she said, "John and I and the entire cast have decided it is true. . . . You really are a witch."

Not long after that, I went to a lovely baby shower, where many wondered out loud what my next spell might be.

As it turned out it would start in the late 1980s, during a roundtable discussion about introducing a new young female character. We had lost Jenny Gardner (the actress who played her, Kim Delaney, had wanted to try her luck in Hollywood). I wanted someone who would come into Pine Valley and cause a lot of problems, especially for herself. Her name would be Hayley Vaughan, and she would be Trevor Dillon's niece. We chose to use Trevor as her uncle because we knew we were underutilizing the talented actor James Kiberd. There would be a lot of potential for emotionally explosive scenes between the two characters.

The network seemed to agree with our new character but turned against us when they read the audition scene with Hayley's characteristics spelled out.

The head of ABC Daytime met with me to voice her objections. She said, "Hayley is too tempestuous. This will turn the audience against her."

"Tempestuous? Really?" I replied.

"Absolutely! You have to change her," she insisted.

"I'm glad you weren't around when the network greenlighted the show. I would have had to fight you for Erica Kane!"

I won that skirmish, and the casting call for the part of seventeen-year-old Hayley was answered by many hopeful and talented actresses. Those who were asked back for the final call included the effervescent eighteen-year-old Kelly Ripa. When the director asked Kelly to tell us a little about herself, she replied that she'd only had a few small roles, but explained, "I've come here because I'm the person you need to play this part. And I know that I will knock your socks off." I knew right then that she was our Haley.

After her arrival in Pine Valley, smack in the center of her uncle Trevor's life, Hayley weathered myriad behavior problems stemming from her drinking, including the realization that as the daughter of the drunken Arlene Vaughan, her alcoholism could have been genetic. Yet even with her own alcoholism identified and treated, Hayley was stalled in that limbo between adolescence and young adulthood, unable to sustain lasting romantic connections.

One of my favorite urgings to our roundtable was "When

in doubt, go deeper"—in other words, find critical "vertical scenes" that reveal the iceberg under the water. One of our writers, Hal Corley, began to look more fully at Hayley's intimacy issues. Where did they come from? The key was the dynamic with her mother.

Engaged to duplicitous Alec McIntyre (the darkly charismatic Grant Aleksander), Hayley neared her own wedding not with joyous anticipation but fearful of the emotional demands the role of wife would place upon her. When Arlene showed up, traumatic memories were triggered. Ignoring her daughter's boundaries from early childhood, the lonely Arlene had long used her as a sounding board, subjecting Hayley to years of inappropriate details about her own promiscuity and unachieved desires. Hayley had been raised in an environment that left her unable to fully form her own identity, so tethered was she to Arlene. It was a difficult series of epiphanies to dramatize—internal psychological revelations always are—but we worked hard to find present-day demonstrations of Hayley's uncovered angst. We asked ourselves, "How would this be manifested? Acted out?"

I remember one telling episode. Hayley had a full-blown panic attack in a dress shop fitting room as she contemplated married life and remembered her mother's lurid tales. Arlene misread Hayley's panic as ordinary cold feet. Instead of helping her weigh serious second thoughts, she pushed Hayley closer to the altar with almost pornographic fervor, insisting she was about to experience life's physical and emotional highs. Once again, the line between Arlene and her daughter blurred; Arlene's projection onto Hayley paralyzed her. Just as Hayley was forced to live through her mother's experiences, Arlene seized her daughter's moment by "coaching" Hayley about her upcoming honeymoon with wild inappropriateness. In truth, we were dramatizing the impact of covert incest—a parent emotionally abusing his or her child by demanding unhealthy intimacy.

When Arlene finally set her sights on Hayley's fiancé, culminating in a blackmail-and-seduction subplot, we brought Hayley's past fully into her present. It was one of the most challenging stories we did during the summer and fall of 1995, and it gave Kelly and the wonderful Olivia Birkelund, as Arlene, some of their most complex scenes. Kelly gave unstintingly, her work specific and nuanced. It was time for Hayley to find the love of her life with Mateo, so she could finally begin exorcising these demons. It would be her powerful transition into an adult character.

It was a tough story arc to sell and make clear to the network. The "root for" wasn't a traditional romantic solution; it was focused on a young woman coming to terms with the true source of her anxiety. Thus it was crucial that for the character of Mateo, we find an actor with whom she would have perfect chemistry.

One day when Kelly was in makeup, a fellow actress rushed in with some news.

"There is one major stud muffin auditioning to play your boyfriend."

The makeup artist was happy to let Kelly out of the chair. A few minutes later Kelly came back to report.

"Major understatement! His name is Mark. I sure hope he gets the part!"

Of course Mark Consuelos did get the part, and soon everyone in production, and the fans, were talking about the electric chemistry between Hayley and Mateo. I began to think I noticed a new light in Kelly's eyes, as well.

We went on location to Jamaica, where the story centered

on Hayley and Mateo's romance. The crew suspected that something stronger was going on between the two actors than just our words in the scripts. A few months later, many were surprised but delighted when Mark and Kelly announced they had eloped and married in Las Vegas. I too was thrilled, but not all that surprised. It had played out just as I'd written it!

ALONG WITH THE extraordinary cast of actors I was so fortunate to work with each day, I also had the chance to have some very special guests on my shows over the years. In the winter of 1973, Susan Lucci and I were on a train to Baltimore to appear on the network television show of a young African-American woman whose program was increasing in popularity. That visit became the basis of a warm relationship between Oprah Winfrey and *All My Children,* on which she later appeared as a newscaster.

Oprah became a rabid fan of *All My Children,* and in the fall of 1995, she invited me and twelve cast members to Chicago to be her guests. Although we didn't have a chance to spend much time together, it always meant a lot to me and, I think, to her. We were both too busy to plan a get-together, but I always loved it when we would meet by chance from time to time. For instance, one time I was on the elevator at Saks and someone poked me in the rib. I turned, and, to my surprise, there she was grinning at me. It took all my self-control to keep from shouting, "Oprah!" I think that like me, she realizes that she was given a gift with her talent, and maybe that's why I always felt we had a connection.

I was also so lucky to cross paths with the wonderful Carol Burnett. I fell in love with Burnett's comic genius the first time I heard her sing, "I fell in love with John Foster Dulles," on *The*

*Garry Moore Show.* When Carol eventually got her own show, I was a loyal fan. Her takeoff on *Gone with the Wind,* when she played Scarlett, wearing her mama's curtains with the rod across her shoulder blades, had me in stitches. I was more than delighted when I heard she was a fan of *All My Children* and that she wanted to play a part on the show.

I didn't realize just how big a fan she was until we met on the set. Carol told me that, while on vacation in Italy, she'd instructed someone on her staff to wire her every day about what happened on the show. One day, that assistant went to her husband and said, "I really don't think we should show this wire to Ms. Burnett, because I think it will upset her to hear Jenny died and Grandma Kate is very sick."

For her role on *AMC,* we cast Carol as Verla Grubbs. While growing up a carny child, Verla never knew the identity of her biological father. Having heard through the carny grapevine that their sideshow went bankrupt performing in Pine Valley, Verla returned to town to look up her old friend the gypsy fortuneteller, now Myrtle Fargate—played by the wonderful Eileen Herlie—who proved to be a gold mine of information. I loved writing scenes between Carol and Eileen.

A humorous twist had Verla taking away Opal Gardner's boyfriend, Sam Brady. In an episode years later, Opal turned the tables and snatched Sam back. Verla put up a brave front and wished them all the happiness in the world. However, once Carol was off-screen, due to her magnificent immersion in her character, we heard her crying her heart out.

Another amusing behind-the-scenes incident occurred when Verla and Myrtle were having lunch at the Château. An obstreperous cleaning woman with a string mop came up to Carol and said, "I knew your mother." Verla replied politely, "How nice." On the close-up of the cleaning woman, the audience could see that it was Elizabeth Taylor, who had orchestrated the surprise for her good friend Carol.

And then there was February 12, 1988, the night before the lighting of the torch that would launch the Winter Olympics in Calgary, which ABC was broadcasting. Tom Murphy, the president of Capital Cities (a large communications company that had acquired ABC in 1985), had invited Bob and me to view the games as his guests. On the first evening, he gave a private dinner. Leading me to a table, he said, "I've seated you next to Warren Buffett. You know Warren, don't you?"

"Only by reputation," I replied. The world's richest man, who had bankrolled the takeover of ABC, had created thousands of millionaires through his financial wizardry. How could I talk to him for a whole evening? Just balancing my checkbook was a challenge.

Warren pulled out the chair next to him, greeted me warmly, and asked, "How's your show going? Tom told me how important you are to ABC. What's interesting to you in your work?" Warren asked.

I replied, "The characters and what drives them." Warren asked which character was driven hardest by wanting money. I replied, "Adam Chandler, and he has a lot of money."

Warren said, "Does it make him happy?"

I said, "Quite the contrary."

To which Warren said, "Is that the theme for *All My Children*?"

And I said, "Yes, and I wish you could play one of the parts."

To which he replied, "When do you want me?"

Beginning in 1992, Warren Buffett played himself as a financial adviser to Erica Kane. He counseled her about opening her own cosmetic business, and in subsequent years, he offered personal advice on her love life and even helped her endure her prison sentence by playing bridge. I will never forget the day in the studio when he insisted on redoing a scene. When Warren asked for a retake, it was because he honestly felt he did not portray his part as he should have. He turned to the director and said, "I really muffed that scene. I want to do it over." The director said it was terrific and that we didn't need a retake. But Warren was adamant because, in his heart, he knew he could have done it better. "Please, do me a favor and retake the scene," he said.

So I went up to the director and said, "You'd better retake it." The director said, "If we do, it's going to take this crew into overtime. Do you want that?" I said, "Do you want Warren to take back his five hundred fifty million dollars?" And so the scene was reshot. Warren was terrific and was pleased. It's a typical example of who Warren Buffett is—determined to do the best he can for everyone. We didn't feel we should challenge Warren if he wanted to work a little harder for his AFTRA card.

Over the years, Bob and I became friends with Warren and his wife, Astrid. Our friendship has been a treasured gift. Some years I only get to see them at the Berkshire Hathaway shareholders' meeting in May, but knowing they are my friends makes my life so much richer.

SOMETIMES THE ACTORS gave such brave performances that they inspired me. In 1995, we developed a new story revolving around Michael Delaney, who soon after arriving in town was considered the best history teacher at Pine Valley High. His thorough knowledge of and passion for history led most students to sign up for his classes, especially modern history. In his lectures on the various important events of that time, he seemed to live the experiences vicariously, making his students share the feeling. As he lectured on Nazi Germany and the conditions of those persecuted, he was so caught up in the subject that he announced that if he had been living then, he would have had to wear a pink badge as a gay man. It was the first anyone in the Valley knew of Michael's sexual orientation, and residents of Pine Valley reacted in extremely negative ways.

Michael was finally vindicated, but as the fictional story ended, a behind-the-camera, true-life drama came to light. When Chris Bruno, the actor, went to audition for the part of Michael Delaney, he had no idea who the character was and became conflicted when told. Chris had to fight his own initial discomfort about playing the part of a man he felt was living an unacceptable lifestyle. But as the plot developed and Chris's outlook on life expanded, his attitude changed completely.

At the annual GLAAD (Gay and Lesbian Alliance Against Defamation) Gala, Chris Bruno received an award for his portrayal of Michael Delaney. When he accepted it, he gave a very moving speech describing his early homophobia and the transformation he underwent while playing Michael. I did not know when Chris started playing the part that he was homophobic, but I was entranced by his acceptance speech. I remember thinking how good an actor he was, and I thanked him for his honesty and integrity. To hear Chris's beautiful speech made me so grateful that we'd created a gay character. As I looked across the table, so proud of our team, I caught the eye of one of our finest writers, Fred Johnson, who had encouraged me to write the story line. It was a true victory for him.

Chris's story also reminds me of another instance where our actors gave such brave performances that they inspired our writing team and me. In 1998, at the Emmy Awards, I started thinking about how we could also bring a lesbian character onto *All My Children*. The makings for the Bianca story began in 1947, when I was nineteen and my college housemate "came out" to me.

Because I wanted the impact to be as meaningful as possible, I knew the lesbian character who came out would have to be Erica's daughter. She would showcase the reactions that many parents have upon finding out that their child is gay or lesbian. I think the right word for Erica's reaction is *denial*. In this prejudicial society in which we live, the first reaction from a parent usually is, "What did I do wrong?" I felt I could help people look at things in a different way.

The dramatic "coming out" scene between Erica and Bianca features a daughter who wants to be seen for the first time, and a mother who wants to remain blind to the truth:

BIANCA: Look at me.

ERICA: I don't want to look at you I want you to go—

BIANCA: Look at me! I want you to see who I am, mother. C-can you see who I am? Can you? I'm trying to show you.

ERICA: Honey, there is something wrong. There is something terribly wrong with you.

BIANCA: No, no, you just won't look.

Finally, it culminates in an emotional revelation that remains one of the most memorable moments from *All My Children:*

BIANCA: Have you always loved me, mom?! Have you?

ERICA: How could you even ask me a question like that?

BIANCA: Do you love me now?

ERICA: Bianca!

BIANCA: Do you . . . ?

ERICA: Yes!

BIANCA: (voice cracking) I'm gay.

*Looks exchanged between the two as silence grows*

**Fade to black**

I knew the audience would stay tuned to follow how Erica would react—and react she did. Initially, Erica's having a lesbian daughter upset a significant portion of the audience. Viewers were deeply attached to the character as the sixteen-year-old daughter of the leading soap opera diva. ABC held a series of focus groups to gauge audience reaction. Female viewers in Boston and some in Atlanta found the story line "refreshing and reflective" of what they called the "real world and its diversity." However, in the Atlanta group, good portions were concerned about morality and did not want a major character "saddled with a lifelong problem." Boston's viewers felt Bianca's problem was being in the closet; Atlanta's said her problem was her sexual preference itself. In addition, there was opposition to the groundswell of support for the character. Critics of gay marriage complained about a sympathetic gay heroine, saying Bianca made daytime television even more licentious.

Bianca's romantic pairing with Lena Kundera resulted in American daytime's first lesbian kiss, which received substantial media attention. The following year, in 2004, Eden Riegel, who played Bianca so beautifully, appeared on the cover of *Girlfriends,* North America's only lesbian monthly magazine; the piece itself discussed Riegel's breakthrough lesbian role. Erin's portrayal of the character incited mania, admiration, and even overprotectiveness from viewers for the character. Riegel additionally won praise from leading gay groups for her "complex portrayal" of Bianca, which many said was groundbreaking. Bianca emerged as a gay icon, with Patrick Healy in the *New York Times* citing her as the first lead character on a major daytime drama to be a lesbian. What I loved about his article was the acknowledgment that during a period when people were "choosing sides over gay marriage and arguing about campaign references to Vice President Dick Cheney's openly gay daughter," our story was reaching people "across the ideological spectrum."

ONE OF THE most inspiring moments I shared with our actors came when Susan Lucci did not win an Emmy after her eighteenth nomination. Everybody was caught up in the drama of when she would finally get her long-deserved award and how she would possibly cope with another rejection. But after another loss, Susan sought me out to say, "I'm over being upset. I want you to know that had I won, I planned to thank you for creating Erica, the greatest role I've had the privilege of playing."

When she finally did win her Emmy in 1999, she thanked me from the stage, saying I had changed the face of daytime television. Bob and I gave a celebratory dinner in her honor at the "21" Club in New York. We invited the whole cast. Many toasts were made to Susan and to me. It was a great joy to see such talent gathered in the room—talent that was devoted to my real world of make-believe. Although she portrayed a vixen who pursued her whims regardless of who might be in her way, the loving wife, mother, and grandmother Susan Lucci has been a treasure as a friend and an incomparable actress.

To tell the truth, the rest of the cast were as superlative as Susan Lucci in their talents. Their loving friendship made us a true family, and that above all else was what made the actors so special to me. In addition, the closeness was why I was worried by what I saw as increasingly poor decisions by network executives concerned about the rise of cable and online streaming options. I told the cast that no matter how they hurt the show, nothing lasted forever, and they would never destroy my beautiful memories of our family.

# Chapter 20

# TIME AND TIDE

Grandma Dalton had a favorite Irish warning: "Coming events cast their shadow."

I often remembered that adage. For many years at *AMC,* we were our own little happy team of writers who turned over our work to an equally gifted production staff and wonderful actors. When the show went to an hour, it seemed to become executive-heavy. Apparently the network's feeling was, the more people who were working on it, the more viewers it would garner.

Actually, the end result was destruction. For example, at an ABC function, a woman came up to my husband and introduced herself as a new ABC employee. She explained she was put in charge of getting rid of that "damn Bible," referring to the large, Bible-like family album that opened every episode. Her tenure was the beginning of the end of our show.

All of these new executives wanted to prove how important they were. They went to our script meetings with their own suggestions for changes. When we disagreed with them, explaining that dialogue came directly from the motivation in the outline, their solution was to attend outline meetings. This caused a lot of confusion on the studio floor. Seasoned actors were disturbed by the motivational changes in their dialogue given by the "suits." To answer the actors' questions, a writer

who was brought in to replace me—after I was pushed out—
told them bluntly, "I don't believe in characters having a lot of
motivation. You're just supposed to speak the lines I give you."

One wonders if that was what motivated him to have a tornado that cost millions to produce. No story followed this cata-
strophic event. Another edict by a male executive with a fondness
for two young actresses led him to insist they be brought into a
plotline in which they had no emotional involvement.

In 2011, the curtain came down on both *All My Children* and
*One Life to Live.* Both companies were as despondent as I was.
My own children were a great comfort to me, and I also spent
hours on the phone grieving with the cast and crew. No more,
"Make 'em laugh, make 'em cry, make 'em wait." No more trying to hold a mirror up to life. To distract myself from the shock
of the cancellation, I glanced at the Emmy statuette given to me
in 1992 for Lifetime Achievement by the National Academy of
Television Arts and Sciences. On its base is inscribed: "Agnes
Nixon introduced social relevance to Daytime, and at the same
time changed traditional storytelling."

Before long, it was time to tape the final episode. *All My
Children* would come to a close after 11,210 episodes across
forty-one years. We made sure that a good many of the *AMC*
cast members would be in the final episode. I flew to New
York to be with them on the studio floor.

I asked them all to sit down near me. I said, "We are in a
very sad moment in our lives. I can't make it any easier for you,
or for myself. In my sadness, what I have been trying to do is
go back in memory to the wonderful times we had as a family.
To the love and care we all shared with each other. There is so
much to remember. Try to keep in the forefront of your minds
that it is not what we have lost but what we've managed to
accomplish that we should treasure. I want to thank each one

of you for being part of our family, and for the way you have touched our fans and even helped a few people along the way."

Suddenly someone started singing the Irish lullaby "Too-Ra-Loo-Ra-Loo-Ral" as tears began to flow. Soon we were all singing, and it was very healing.

Despite the pain, we all knew that forty-one years is a good run, and it leaves me with memories and gratitude that can never die and with friends and colleagues whom I shall never forget. I am grateful to the networks, particularly ABC, for allowing me to dramatize the many problems that haunt our society today. I always hoped the stories would be helpful to some in the audience.

Nor will I forget Mrs. Quakenbush, the Davenport psychic who, many years ago, warned me not to be too proud or puffed up and to always remember my responsibility to those who were watching.

I still live in the same house Bob and I bought almost fifty years ago. My life today is so enriched by my children, grandchildren, and great-grandchildren that I am so thankful that I was determined to have children and a career. As season follows season, I increasingly empathize with the events of my children's lives. By this point, my children had long been adults, and my grandchildren were well on their way. I live for visits from them and my three great-grandchildren.

My only regret is that Bob is not here to enjoy them with me today. It's hard to believe we lost him to cancer on November 22, 1996, when he was seventy-five. He was a wonderful father and a loving husband with legions of friends whose lives he enriched. People sometimes ask if I thought it was difficult for him to be married to one of the first successful women working in what was then a man's world. I say, "Yes, I'm sure at times it was hard as hell. That's why Bob Nixon is a woman's lib hero." I explained that, many times, some Neanderthal would tease him about "letting" his wife work. Or about the fact that his wife made more money than he did. But I was very lucky. The day he proposed, Bob said he would support my writing career, and he always did, in good times and bad. We often referred to our marriage as a partnership. I knew how lucky I was, and I think Bob felt the same way.

One thing Bob and I always promised each other was that we would travel to the far places we yearned to see when we reached our golden years. Unfortunately we were denied that, but I continue to travel with our children and grandchildren, and I always feel that Bob is on the trip with us.

My apartment in New York City enables me to spend time with very dear friends whom I have met along the way. Lola Finkelstein lives in the apartment below mine, and during our frequent visits, we are so close that we often joke that we feel like long-lost sisters.

Three years ago, I woke up on the floor of my apartment and discovered I could not move. The ER doctor delivered the terrifying news that I had suffered a stroke. As I lay on the stretcher wondering if I was going to live or die, he told me they were preparing me for a CAT scan to determine the extent of the damage. Sedatives put me to sleep, and I was awakened by voices saying, "Mom . . . Aggie . . ."

When I opened my eyes, my children and grandchildren were standing around my bed, and I felt a great sense of peace. As we waited seven tense hours for the doctor to deliver the verdict, my family never meant so much to me. Suddenly the doctor appeared.

"You're one lucky lady because you were brought to the ER so fast. You didn't even need the medicine that dissolves blood clots. Your body is doing that on its own. I'm going to let nature take its course and not do anything invasive."

Nature, and two years of hard work and determination in therapy, have me returning to the life I thought I had lost. To anyone who thinks they may be having a stroke, please get to a hospital right away. Time makes all the difference; an hour or two can be a matter of life and death. Every day, I'm so grateful for the immediate help that allowed me to open my eyes and see my children smiling at me.

I also love the way in which my career has allowed me to develop such deep friendships with the wonderful actors who have brought my characters to life. For instance, Susan Lucci and her husband, Helmut, are dear friends. Two years after my stroke, I was so happy that we could again go out to dinner in New York. We were both feeling sentimental as we settled into our seats at Café Boulud and talked about our wonderful collaboration.

Suddenly, Susan started motioning as if she were applying eye makeup. My confusion evaporated as soon as she started speaking: Instantly she became sixteen-year-old Erica Kane, defending her before-school application of mascara. "Mother, of course I'm wearing mascara to school. Don't be silly. I'm not wearing it for Philip Brent. I'm wearing it for my geometry teacher; I'm doing awfully. But you're right about one thing. Philip would rather look at me than that boring Tara Martin."

My eyes welled up as I remembered first seeing the audition tape of Susan bringing my dialogue to life and knowing we had found Erica Kane. A teary Susan said, "I've never forgotten the audition scene. You wrote it so perfectly. It just captured the mother-daughter relationship. I had never read such authentic dialogue, and I was desperate to play Erica. Thank you for everything, Aggie."

Recently, the wonderful Julia Barr and I had dinner at my apartment. We were reminiscing about the stories on the show. Julia brought up how we dramatized the tragedy of drunk driving and repeated what her character, Brooke English, said when she heard her little girl was killed by a drunken driver: "I have to go to be with Laura. She's so afraid of the dark."

As she did in the original episode, Julia conveyed the anguish of the devastated mother. It broke my heart all over again. I told Julia she had a great talent that could make us both cry and laugh.

Now I divide my time between family and friends, and a new kind of writing. I also have to find time for physical and speech therapy, but my love of writing still dominates my life. I'm now working on ideas for a series of short stories.

People still ask me, "How did you ever do it?" This brings me back to that moment when Barbara Walters asked me the same question. I do feel lucky that despite so many people who tried to stand in my way—including my father—I was able to continue writing, creating characters, and inventing stories. I'm also proud to have helped launch so many acting careers through daytime television.

Recently I visited an entire Connecticut warehouse filled with tens of thousands of my scripts. It strengthened my feeling that it all came from my unnamed, unlettered long-ago Irish ancestor whose stories mesmerized her family as they huddled around the peat fire.

I have come to see what people mean when they say that I have a very good memory. Sometimes I'm not sure if it's a gift or a curse. You cannot know what you've forgotten, but I believe I may remember all the conversations and all the dialogue that I've ever heard. That's weird, I know. My patient husband would often kid me about it, recalling the time I wanted to talk about a dinner we'd had years before at the "21" Club in New York.

I said, "Of course you remember, Bob. You wore the camel-hair jacket I bought you for Christmas. It looked so good with the brown knit tie and brown slacks. And Lou Weiss said how nice it looked. Don't you remember that?"

Bob replied, "No, Ag, I don't remember, and I'll be damned if I'm going to try."

But it's more than memory. I feel a space in my brain, a room where writing ideas are born. I don't think of stories. Instead, I hear voices—people in scenes talking to each other or someone speaking to me. My whole life, I've felt compelled to put them on paper. That is why I had no choice but to be a writer. And I have loved every minute of it.

# AFTERWORD

Throughout our lives, when fans would thank our mother for her writing, Ag would always say, "If I have any talent I don't deserve any credit. It is God given. I will take credit for one thing: putting the seat of my pants in the seat of my chair."

Ag's tens of thousands of hours of television are proof that beneath her slight, elegant, and friendly persona she possessed a steely discipline. But the warehouse full of her scripts at Northwestern University and the University of Pennsylvania's Annenberg School for Communication are also testament to the immense joy she found in writing. She often admitted she lived in two worlds: the real world and her real world of make-believe. No one in her family, and few who knew her, would deny that, while she loved us all deeply, we were in stiff competition with her friends and her other "family" living in Pine Valley and Llanview.

So when, after four decades, ABC canceled both her shows on the same day, it was a tough blow. But before long, she got to work on this memoir. It was something she had always wanted to do, but that had been beyond even her superhuman capacity, with two hours of television a day to produce.

So she put the seat of her pants back in the seat of her chair and began to write her story. For someone who found writing so easy, she found the new format a surprising challenge.

Several people suggested hiring a "ghostwriter," which was shot down immediately. She would be writing every word! Ag quickly fell in love with writing this memoir and put her heart and soul into it.

Then, four years ago, our mother suffered a debilitating stroke. She worked extremely hard at her rehab and speech therapy, and all of her children were fine with the knowledge that her motivation was not just to be with us, but to get back to work! Her limited mobility during her recovery quickly forced this book to become a family affair. Ag needed all hands on deck to translate her chicken scratch writing onto the computer or type as she dictated. Every one of our clan, from children to great-grandchildren, made a contribution!

And then there were the unending rewrites upon rewrites. The stroke had impacted her walking and speech, but her mind and wit remained razor-sharp. It became essential and full-time volunteer work, and it was a gift to us. It gave us a remarkable window into the life of this dynamic woman, but also into almost a century of American history. For the son who so admired his mother's gifts, the biggest reward was sitting next to her—or on a cell phone, while in the middle of a film shoot miles offshore—madly typing as she dictated. In every session she would deliver a great piece of writing, and Bob would always say the same thing: "You might only weigh eighty pounds, but you've still got your fastball."

One thing that surprised her was how much detail was required for a book compared to television. Ag loved working with Matt Inman, her editor at Crown, but was at first taken aback by how much detail he pushed for, and the volume of comments he put in the margins of her manuscript. But we worked through them one by one over the course of more than a year. On Sunday, September 28, knowing the finish line was in sight, we worked for seven hours straight. Finally we were down to Matt's final comment: "MI: People might be interested in why you chose the title *One Life to Live*. What did it mean to you?"

Ag gazed out the window for a long time and dictated this answer:

> I finally had the perfect title for it: *One Life to Live*. All my life, it had been a passion of mine, a basic truth: we only have one life to live, and we have to try to make the most out of it. As my babies came along, I was even more obsessed with the brevity of life and how little time we have. I wanted to help other people understand how to make our brief candle burn brightly with a light that shines on the path of life.

Yet again she earned Bob's oft-used line. "You might only weigh eighty pounds, but you've still got your fastball."

We celebrated her writing the last words of her beloved memoir as she booked a hair appointment and started planning her book tour. It was the furthest from any of our minds that they would be the last words she ever wrote. It was a crushing shock when our beloved mother died in her sleep two days later.

It's no coincidence that our mother passed away just a couple days after her memoir was complete. And although she had no plans of dying, ever, her health was so precarious the last year, it's a testament to her love of this project that through sheer force of will she saw it through to the very end. From start to finish, the process of documenting her life story became a way for her to connect with her family. From suffering over the structure of a single sentence to endlessly sorting through photos from ninety-two years of baptisms, birthday parties, weddings, graduations, and vacations, the book in many ways was a collaborative effort and that pleased Mom immensely. So while *My Life to Live* is important on its own as a great story, we her family feel its true value lies in the satisfaction its creation brought to her final years. Her beloved creations fell victim to the changing world of network television and her mobility became increasingly limited, but having this sense of purpose made her part of the world outside and gave her a reason to soldier on. We could have asked for nothing more.

—Bob and Emily Nixon

# THE NORTHWESTERN UNIVERSITY
# RADIO PLAY SHOP

TITLE: NO FLAGS FLYING

AUTHOR: Agnes Eckhardt, Spring 1944

ANNOUNCER: Ladies and gentlemen, this afternoon we are paying a visit to a home. An average-sized home in an average-sized town in the average-sized state of Iowa. We walk up the green lawn, pat the German police dog that lies on the porch, and enter the redbrick house. We go up the stairs to a small, den-like room, the walls adorned with many college letters and ribbons. To the left, Mr. O'Brien is seated before a large box he seems to be sorting. (VOICE FADES)

FATHER: Yes, I was just taking this Sunday off to go through a box of my son's souvenirs and sort 'em out. (SHORT LAUGH) When he left for the Air Corps he was so excited, he didn't put anything much in order. I remember he said though, "Don't throw any of those things away, Dad. They're all awfully important. Save 'em for me!" I guess you know how it is if you have a son. So I just thought I'd make this box look a little less like something the cat dragged in. You don't mind if I just go on while you're here, do you? You can pull up that footstool if you'd care to. It's over there, under that autographed picture of Frankie Parker.

(SOFT CHUCKLE) Now, who'd ever have thought

Tim would be keeping this baby picture of himself? Think I'll just hang it up. It's painted on ivory in oils. I had it done as a surprise for Mother. Yeah, he was just five at the time. Certainly shows up that mass of black ringlets and blue eyes, doesn't it? He was an Irishman from the very beginning. Golly, I remember the day this was taken. Just after the three little fellows, Tim, the oldest mind you, had had an argument about an old swing I'd made for them from a discarded tire. (VOICE FADES)

SOUND: VOICES OF THREE CHILDREN ALL YELLING AT ONCE.

TIM: (ABOVE THE OTHERS) I wanna swing! I wanna! You let me!

BOB & ED: (FOUR AND THREE) No! No! No! Me! Me!

FATHER: (COMING ON MIKE) Here, here! What's all this trouble?

TIM: Daddy, make Ed and Bob let me swing. I wanta swing!

ED: I haven't had my turn!

BOB: Yes, you have, Ed. Yes you have!

ALL: (AGAIN GENERAL PANDEMONIUM) I wanna swing! Let me! Make him let me, Daddy!

FATHER: (ABOVE THE DIN) Now just a minute! This is terrible! A disgrace! Don't you know you can't do this? You can't possibly cry in that swing!

ALL: (CRYING SUBSIDES TO FEW WHIMPERS)

*Later,*

TIM: Why?

BOB: Why, Daddy?

ED: Why?

FATHER: Good heavens! You mean you don't know?

ALL BOYS: (NOW REALLY CURIOUS) No!

FATHER: To think you've been swinging in this swing for almost two months, almost an age! And you never knew that this is a laughing swing.

TIM: A laughin' swing?

ED: Laughin' swing?

BOB: What's a laughin' swing?

FATHER: Yes, indeed, a laughing swing. And you only find them once every so often. No one can ever swing in that swing without laughing. (STARTS TO LAUGH) (FROM OFF MIKE A BIT) Look! I can't even go near it without laughing.

TIM: (CATCHING THE SPIRIT) A laughin' swing! A laughin' swing!

ED & BOB: (BOTH START TO LAUGH): Yeah, a laughin' swing! You go now, Timmy.

ALL BOYS: (LAUGHING TOGETHER)

SOUND: THE ROPE ATTACHED TO THE TIRE TWISTS AS THE TIRE SWINGS BACK AND FORTH ON THE LIMB. MIXED WITH CHILDREN'S LAUGHTER. FADES.

FATHER: (FADING IN) Guess you don't see laughing swings made out of tires these days, eh? Now what in time is this old chewing gum wrapper doing here? Certainly looks worn, doesn't it? (PAUSE) Say, you know what? This must be a souvenir from Tim's first airplane ride when he was ten. We were spending the summer at Lake Gogebic. It was . . . (FADES OUT)

SOUND: AIRPLANE MOTOR FADES IN SLIGHTLY.

FATHER: Tim persuaded his mother to take him up in one of those old-time aquaplanes that took ten-minute sightseeing tours. (VOICE FADES)

SOUND: BUILDS AND FADES QUICKLY. MOTOR UNDER ENTIRE SCENE.

MOTHER: Timothy, you must sit down!

TIM: Look, Mom! There's our cabins! See 'em!

MOTHER: Yes, dear, I see them.

TIM: (VERY EXCITED) Those sailboats look like my toy one, don't they! You see 'em, Mom? See 'em over there?

MOTHER: Oh, my, yes, Timothy! Please don't make Mother ask you to stay in your seat again, dear!

TIM: Golly gee! I wish I could fly. That's what I'll be someday. You wait and see. Someday, I'll be a pilot. Only my ship'll be lots bigger and go lots higher and faster than this one! You wait and see! Golly gee! (VOICE FADES)

SOUND: AIRPLANE MOTOR UP AND FADE OUT

FATHER: (FADES IN) We didn't pay any attention to him then, but I guess Tim knew what he wanted, all right. Who'd have thought . . . ? Well, well! The rabbit's foot from the radiator cap of Tim's old model T2 we gave him for his sixteenth birthday. (FADES)

SOUND: BOYISH FOOTSTEPS RUNNING DOWNSTAIRS.

MOTHER: Good morning, Tim. Happy birthday, dear!

TIM: (NOW SIXTEEN) Thanks, Mom!

ED & BOB: (FIFTEEN AND FOURTEEN) Yeah, happy birthday, old man!

TIM: Where did you get that!

SOUND: FOOTSTEPS

FATHER: Well, happy birthday, Tim!

TIM: Thanks, Dad!

FATHER: I picked a little something up for you in town, son, but I'm sorry I didn't have time to wrap it. Mother didn't think you'd mind though.

TIM: (EXPECTING TO RECEIVE IT THEN) No, that's okay.

MOTHER: We left it outside, son.

ED: (DYING TO TELL HIM) Go over to the window and look!

BOB: Yeah! Take a gander!

SOUND: FOOTSTEPS TO WINDOW.

TIM: (ENTHUSIASTICALLY) Hey! You don't mean! . . .
Hey, is it really mine? The car, I mean!

FATHER: All yours, son!

BOB: Isn't it a smoothie!

ED: Well, come on, Tim, let's go see it!

TIM: Yeah!

SOUND: RACING FOOTSTEPS. SLAM OF DOOR. FOOT-
STEPS DOWN CONCRETE STEPS.

TIM: Golly! What a beauty! No top! And a crank! Just the
way I wanted!

SOUND: HONK OF VERY CRUDE, OLD-FASHIONED HORN.

TIM: Ah! Music to my ears! Gee, thanks, Mom and
Dad! Gee!

FATHER: Glad you like it, Tim.

MOTHER: But you will be careful, dear?

TIM: Sure!

BOB: What will you call it, Tim?

TIM: Uh, let's see. Got to get a good name. Why, I got it,
"Frankie Parker."

ED: Hey, that's good! We'll have to hit over the radio with
a Coke to christen it!

BOB: Frankie Parker! Boy!

TIM: Well, come on! What are we waiting for? Let's go
over twelve. And pick up Spike and Butch.

SOUND: SCRAMBLING INTO CAR DURING NEXT FEW LINES.

ED: And Muggs and Flash.

TIM: Boy, will we have the times!

SOUND: NOISIEST OF MOTORS. CAR STARTS CHUGGING DOWN THE STREET AT A RAPID CLIP.

BOYS: Bye, Dad! Bye, Mom!

MOTHER: Timothy, do be careful.

TIM: (SHOUTING BACK) We will!

SOUND: DISTANT BLAST FROM THE OLD HORN.

MOTHER: Dad, we'll be sorry for this yet!

SOUND: CAR FADES OUT.

FATHER: (FADING IN) But Tim was careful, (CHUCKLE) with a few minor exceptions. He had that car apart every day and twice on Sunday. And he finally sold it for more than we paid for it!

Here's something you might be interested in, too. Picture of Tim's track team in prep school back east. He was captain his senior year. That's Tim with the winged foot sketched under him. That was always sort of his symbol, the winged foot. For speed, you know. One time his mother and I went all the way to New York to see him run the Penn Relays at Madison Square Garden.

SOUND: CROWDS CHEERING FADE IN AND HOLD UNDER FOLLOWING SPEECH.

FATHER: (DESCRIPTIVE) Tim was running in the hundred-yard dash.

(EXCITED) Mother and I sat there clutching each other's hands.

MOTHER: He's third in lead, Dad!

FATHER: (IN SUPPRESSED TONES) Take it easy, Tim. Save yourself for the last fifty feet.

MOTHER: I'm almost afraid to look.

FATHER: (ALMOST BEYOND ALL CONTROL HIM-SELF) Now just relax, Mary. Don't get nervous. Easy does it, son! He's going up to second place! Atta boy, Tim! Atta boy!

MOTHER: They are neck and neck. Oh, Dad, they're going to tie.

FATHER: No! No! Look! He did it!

MOTHER: He won! Oh, Dad! He won!

SOUND: CROWDS CHEERING AND CLAPPING.

FATHER: Here he comes running over to us!

SOUND: RUNNING FOOTSTEPS GETTING CLOSER.

FATHER: Nice going, son! Nice going!

MOTHER: You were wonderful, dear!

TIM: (PANTING FOR BREATH) Thanks! Sort of had me—

FATHER: We knew you'd do it, Tim!

MOTHER: (STARTLED) Timothy, what is that on your left arm?

TIM: (EVASIVELY) Where?

MOTHER: You know perfectly well where! Right there!

TIM: (SHEEPISHLY) That? Oh, that's just my winged foot.

MOTHER: (FEARING IT ISN'T) But, is it painted on, Tim?

TIM: Uh, no. A bunch of us had them tattooed on last night. Classy, don't you think, Mom?

MOTHER: Oh, Timothy, a tattoo! (VOICE FADES)

FATHER: (FADES IN) Yes. Mom couldn't get over that tattoo for some time, but it was only a small one, and boys'll be boys, I told her. Lucky it was so little.

(NEW TRAIN OF THOUGHT) Well, I guess this whole section of the box is full of souvenirs from Tim's college years. He left for the service when he was a junior, but the time he did spend at the university was full of excitement. This generation seems to make the best of everything. Look at this initialed sweater. He made varsity football his sophomore year— fishing tackle— old athletic book . . . program for the homecoming game— Here're his dress shoes with his feather carnation and bow tie stuck down in the toe. Boy, how Tim hated to get dressed up for dances. But he met a girl in college, and so he'd take Jeannie to the dances just to keep her from going with anyone else. This lace handkerchief and packet of letters are hers. That was sure a case of love at first sight. This college album is full of Jeannie's pictures.

SOUND: TURNING OF HEAVY PAGES.

FATHER: Before Tim left we were looking through this book and he told me about the different times when these snapshots were taken.

SOUND: TURNING ANOTHER PAGE.

FATHER: Here is a good one of Jeannie. Just the opposite of Tim, small and blonde. Yes, he's a good six feet two. I remember Tim said this one was taken on a picnic. They used to hike out to some grounds and . . . (VOICE FADES)

SOUND: BURNING AND CRACKLING OF OUTDOOR FIRE. SIZZLING OF STEAK.

TIM: (CALLING FROM OFF MIKE) Hey, Jeannie, isn't that steak done yet? I'm hungry!

JEANNIE: Yes, it's ready now, come on! Oh, and Tim, will you bring a couple of more pieces of wood?

TIM: (OFF MIKE) Okay. (COMING ON MIKE, CARRYING WOOD) Here's the wood. (DROPS IT) Hey, does that look good!

JEANNIE: Just wait until you taste it! I'm the best steak fryer in seven counties! Get a roll and I'll put this nice juicy piece in it for you.

TIM: Okay.

JEANNIE: There! Sink your teeth into that, now!

TIM: (TAKING A BITE) Boy! Is this super!

JEANNIE: Pretty good cook, eh?

TIM: Not bad! Not half bad!

JEANNIE: (JOKINGLY) Why, Mr. O'Brien, your flattering overcomes me!

TIM: Say, Jeannie, what are you doing after graduation, for the rest of your life?

JEANNIE: Why, haven't you heard? I'm cooking for you!

BOTH: (LAUGH)

TIM: That sounds wonderful to me. That is if you'll have steak; otherwise, deal's off! (LAUGHS)

JEANNIE: Why, you— Give me back that sandwich, you can't have it!

TIM: (LAUGHING) Get away!

JEANNIE: What a crack!

TIM: Hey! Now look what you made me do! I dropped it on the ground!

BOTH: (LAUGHTER, FADES)

FATHER: (FADES IN) Yes, they had some great times! (LAUGHS) Here's a picture of all of us, taken when Jeannie came home with Tim for Easter vacation. She seemed just like one of the family by this time. Every night the gang of them would go down to the kitchen. They'd end with a startling new milk shake. (VOICE FADES)

TIM: Wonder if there is a cake left.

SOUND: OPENING OF A TIN CAKE CONTAINER. THEN
DROP OF LID.

TIM: Nope, Ed's already been down, once.

ED: Say, you're crazy. I didn't see a crumb of it after dinner.

TIM & ED: Yeah, I'll bet.

JEANNIE: You three bullies stop picking on me. Any day
    I'd get a piece of cake with you wolves around!

BOB: Listen to the girl! I always pass her the food as soon
    as I've finished!

ED: So do I. After me, Jeannie comes first any day in the
    week. And that's how she shows her appreciation!

TIM: Well, we'd better make an "Awful-Awful"!

BOB: Oh, yes we can't neglect our nightly Awful-Awful.

JEANNIE: Not another one tonight!

ED: You mean you don't like them?

JEANNIE: But, you put so much in them!

TIM: Well, that's where the art comes in! The O'Briens are
    the best Awful-Awful makers in Iowa! Bob, get a quart
    of milk.

BOB: Right!

SOUND: FOOTSTEPS. OPENING OF ICEBOX DOOR.

TIM: I'll get the malt and honey.

TIM: I think we ought to put in some vanilla and chocolate tonight, don't you?

ED: Yeah! That really makes it swell!

JEANNIE: Ohhhhhhh!

BOB: Tim, there's some applesauce in the icebox. Think we could use it?

TIM: Yeah, boy! Bring it out!

SOUND: SLAM OF ICEBOX DOOR OFF MIKE. FOOTSTEPS.

BOB: Quart of milk.

ED: Better put in three teaspoons of malt, and two of sugar.

BOB: And here's a pint of vanilla ice cream.

SOUND: ACCOMPANYING SOUNDS TO SUGGEST POUR-ING, STIRRING, ETC.

TIM: Neat!

JEANNIE: Now you all can't possibly drink all that!

TIM: Well! You just wait and see.

ED: I thought we could throw these raisins in for good measure!

TIM: Now vanilla, chocolate. Where's the applesauce, Bob?

BOB: Here!

TIM: Boy! What a drink.

ED: Shall we start her up?

TIM: Seems like we need something else to finish it off, you know?

JEANNIE: (LAUGHS) Finish it off or finish us off?

BOB: I've got it! Some cinnamon!

TIM: Bob, it's plain to see you're the brains of this family. Now that does it! Agreed!

ALL: Rights!

TIM: Let 'er go!

SOUND: CHURNING OF ELECTRIC MIXER.

BOB: (ABOVE THE NOISE) Here are the glasses.

TIM: Okay.

ED: Think it's ready?

TIM: Yeah, I guess so. We don't want the ice cream to melt. Too much.

SOUND: MOTOR STOPS.

TIM: Now where's your glass, Jeannie? You're about to try something you'll never forget!

JEANNIE: (LAUGHING) I'm sure of it!

ED: Well, here's to us!

TIM: Yeah!

BOB: Say, Tim, maybe we didn't need that applesauce after all!

ALL: (LAUGHTER, FADES)

FATHER: (FADES IN) It's been a long time since we've had Awful-Awful lately. . . . Oh, here's a good picture. Was taken at the prom. Tim was telling me it was the first orchid he ever sent a girl. Pretty proud of it, too, but prouder of her, I guess. . . . (FADE)

MUSIC: "INTERMEZZO" IN AND UNDER.

JEANNIE: My orchid is so lovely, Tim.

TIM: You make it look good.

JEANNIE: I know that isn't true, but I like to hear you say it.

TIM: I really like that dress you've got on.

JEANNIE: (LAUGHS SOFTLY) Thank you, darling. It's the same one I've worn to the last three dances. I love this place. Don't you, Tim?

TIM: Yeah. I sort of think of it as belonging especially to us.

JEANNIE: I know.

TIM: Will you miss me when I leave, Jeannie?

JEANNIE: Tim, you know I will. Let's not even think about it—tonight.

TIM: I'll love you for the rest of my life, Jeannie.

JEANNIE: I'll love you, too, darling.

MUSIC: FADES OUT.

TIM: I'll be over tomorrow at one.

BOY: Hey, you two love birds, the music's stopped!

JEANNIE: Oh, Tim, how stupid of us!

BOTH: (LAUGHTER, FADES)

FATHER: (FADES IN) That was Tim's last big college dance. He left for the Air Corps two weeks later. Here's a snapshot of Mom, Jeannie, Tim, and I in front of the post office. That's where they left from. We drove down to Peoria to see him off. I remember how ninety-six young fellows were lined up there. (FADES)

SOUND: VOICES OF MANY BOYS.

SERGEANT: (BOOMING) Quiet! Now, you can talk with your families and friends for a while, but don't leave the Post Office square. When I blow the whistle, you'll all fall into ranks of two and march to the railroad station. Say good-bye to your family here, for ranks will not be broken at the station. We'll get right on the train. And remember! Nobody's wife or sweetheart walks in line with him!

CROWD: (GENERAL LAUGHTER, THEN FADES)

SERGEANT: Okay! Dismissed!

SOUND: SCUFFLING OF FEET.

TIM: Well, looks like I'm in the army!

MOTHER: (TRYING TO KEEP HER VOICE STEADY) What will you do with the suit you're wearing, son?

TIM: I'll send it to you as soon as I get some G.I. duds, Mom.

JEANNIE: We won't know where to write you, Tim.

TIM: No, I won't know where I'm going till I get there. But I'll write anyway, and then mail them when I send you the address.

JEANNIE: Every day!

FATHER: Got enough money, Tim? Can't have you stranded someplace without money for a cup of coffee.

TIM: You've given me money three times already, Dad. Gee, wonder when we're gonna get started—I hate this waiting around.

MOTHER: Do you think you'll get a furlough anytime soon, dear?

TIM: (LAUGHING) You ask the Sergeant that, Mom!

SOUND: SHARP WHISTLE.

SERGEANT: (CALLING OFF MIKE) Fall in!

TIM: Well, I guess that means me. Good-bye, Dad!

FATHER: Good luck, son!

TIM: Thanks.

MOTHER: You will take care of yourself, dear?

TIM: Don't worry, Mom, I'll be okay.

FATHER: Of course you will.

TIM: Good-bye, Jeannie. Don't forget to write.

JEANNIE: Good-bye, darling. I won't forget.

TIM: (SUDDENLY) Well, adios!

SOUND: RAPID FOOTSTEPS.

MOTHER: (SOFTLY) TIM!

FATHER: Now, Mary!

MOTHER: I'm all right, Dad!

JEANNIE: Look, Tim's waving.

ALL: Good-bye, Tim! Bye, son!

SOUND: MARCHING FEET BUILD AND FADE.

FATHER: That was the beginning! My, but we had heart failure several times. Tim was always doing something wrong, and then he'd write and say that the next time we heard from him he'd be washed out. Kept his mother worrying half of every day. This little pink slip reminds me of a time Tim wrote about. It's a sign a cadet made a bad check ride. Tim was in primary training, just been flying a few days . . . (FADES)

SOUND: ROAR OF PLANE MOTOR. WITH MANY DIPS AND ROLLS.

INSTRUCTOR: (ABOVE ROAR OF MOTOR) Keep the nose up. Keep the nose up.

TIM: (YELLING BACK) Yessssir.

INSTRUCTOR: Your right wing is almost perpendicular with the earth. Pull her 'round. Pull her 'round.

TIM: Yessir . . . yesssir.

INSTRUCTOR: Now set her down. Easy! Easy!

SOUND: PLANE LANDS, INDICATING ANYTHING BUT AN "EASY" JOB. CUT MOTOR. CLIMBING OUT OF PLANE.

INSTRUCTOR: (TRYING TO RESTRAIN HIMSELF) Cadet O'Brien!

TIM: (VERY MILITARILY) Yessir! (FADES)

INSTRUCTOR: Cadet O'Brien, I have had one ride in my life worse than this one, (NOW BLEATING IT OUT) and that was with you yesterday!

TIM: Yes, sir! Thank you, sir! Yessir! (FADES)

FATHER: But Tim made it. I knew he would. And then came the final day. He got his wings. He was certainly proud. (CONFIDENTIALLY) Not so proud as his old man, though. We went way out west to see him. Lucky we did, 'cause he never got a furlough. Here is his graduation announcement. Yes sirree, a hundred and ninety men in one month. (VOICE FADES)

OFFICER: (FADES IN, END OF GRADUATION ADDRESS GIVEN OFF MIKE) And so, one hundred and ninety men today have won their wings, their glorious badge of service in the United States Army Air Corps. They're proud, we are proud, our country is proud. To you, brave warriors of the skies, we give you our heartfelt congratulations and every wish for a victorious return!

SOUND: CHEERS AND CLAPPING, FADES TO BACKGROUND.

TIM: (RUNNING ON MIKE) Hey, folks! I got it! I got it!

MOTHER: Oh, Tim, dear.

FAMILY: Congratulations, etc.!

TIM: Did you hear what I said? I got it!

MOTHER: Got what, Tim?

TIM: I've been assigned to a Lightning, Dad!

FATHER: That's great, son.

MOTHER: They go pretty fast, don't they, Tim?

TIM: I'll say! Better than four hundred miles an hour! Boy, was I lucky, though.

FATHER: (FADES IN) He was so very happy. We couldn't act as if we weren't, although our hearts skipped a beat. Guess I'm just an old-timer. Tim and his precious Lightning were soon sent to the Aleutians. They needed men so badly he never got a leave. So a small chain of islands we scarcely knew existed before suddenly became the most important place on the globe.

It's been eight months since he left, hasn't been a word of complaint from Tim. No, sir. Fog up there is pretty dense you know. The fellas don't have much recreation or fresh food, but they sure manage to keep happy it seems. Tim's often written about . . . (FADES)

TIM: (WRITING THE LETTER) (FADES IN) At four a.m. It looks like I might get home by summer. Just in time for your and Dad's twenty-fifth wedding anniversary. That would really be neat, wouldn't it? Has Bob gotten into the Air Corps yet? Tell him to start aiming for a P-38n right away. They're the only ship, believe me! Don't worry about me up here. We get along okay. It would suit me fine except that I'd rather be in the European theater where things are really buzzing. It's kinda like being in the minor leagues. But I guess we can't all play for the big stakes. (VOICE FADES)

FATHER: (FADES IN) I suppose that's the way most oft he feels up there. The thing they are fighting more than anything else is the weather. A twenty-four-hours-a-day enemy. Those williwaws are pretty tricky. Heck, they fight two things at once, the Japs and the weather. (FADES)

MAJOR: (FADES IN) We leave at dawn. Now remember, men, this is an important mission. We're going all the way to the Kuril Islands. It's almost two thousand miles, round-trip. That means the Lightnings will have to carry two five-hundred-gallon tanks of gas for refueling. This is a big job, and the Japs are tricky. They may be expecting us. But I don't have to tell you that they aren't the only thing to worry about. We've got to combat the weather from the beginning of this flight to the end. The forecast reports a fog density from one to ten miles. We may go on instruments almost the entire flight. If we do, spread out. Lightnings take to higher altitudes.

There will be a fleet of destroyers to meet us an hour from Paramushiro Jap Air Base. It is of vital importance that we meet on schedule. Keep your heads and depend only on my direction from Flagship. I say as well that operationally I wouldn't even let you get hours in this sort of fog, but the mission's been planned from headquarters and can't be postponed.

SOUND: RINGING OF ALARM WHISTLE.

MAJOR: Okay, man your ships! Lieutenant O'Brien!

TIM: Yes, sir?

MAJOR: You will lead the formation of Lightnings.

SOUND: ALARM WHISTLES AGAIN. GENERAL HUBBUB OF VOICES AND INSTRUCTIONS.

MIKE: (WHILE RUNNING) Hey, that you, Tim?

TIM: (ALSO RUNNING TO SHIP) Yeah, Mike.

MIKE: Can't see much in this fog.

TIM: It's sure pea soup, all right.

MIKE: I can think of lovelier ways to spend an evening!

TIM: Not getting soft are you? Besides it's not evening but almost dawn.

MIKE: Soft? After eight months in this muck, I'm practically sporous! How can you tell it's dawn, from the sun beating down on your neck!

TIM: Well, here's my ship. I'll meet you in Chicago for the all-star game.

MIKE: It's a date, pal! (LOWER) Well, smooth sailing, chum!

TIM: (ALSO TENSE) Yeah, keep flyin', Mike! (LIGHTLY) And don't be a sky hog if we go on instruments, you Montana cowboy!

MIKE: I'll remember!

SOUND: WHIR OF PROPELLER.

TIM: (CLIMBING INTO SHIP) Adios, Mike!

MIKE: (CALLING BACK) Adios, Tim! Don't forget the all-star game. (FADES OUT)

SOUND: AIRPLANE MOTORS BUILD AND FADE TO BACKGROUND.

MAJOR: (COMING OVER FILTER) This is Major Spaeth, in Flagship. Good work, men. Mission successfully completed. Now three hundred miles southwest of Attu. Lieutenant O'Brien. Calling Lieutenant O'Brien. Are you in formation?

TIM: (OVER FILTERS) Lieutenant O'Brien to Flagship! Roger!

MAJOR: Flagship to O'Brien. How is the fuel supply for Lightnings?

TIM: Lieutenant O'Brien to Flagship. Fuel supply adequate. Sir!

MAJOR: Flagship to squadron! Flagship to squadron! Fog descending. Williwaws! Go on instrument— Spread out— Spread out—Visibility one mile only— Watch your altitude— Lightnings take ten thousand: Go on instrument— Break formation.

SOUND: BUZZING MOTORS BUILD UNDER LAST LINES. UP AND FADES.

SOUND: BUZZING OF VOICES IN FLIGHT ROOM. FADES LOW.

OFFICER: Do you know how it happened, sir?

MAJOR: Collision in mid-air, I guess. Too dense to see anything. They have searched the water for two days, now. But not a trace.

OFFICE: Of all people, Mike and Tim.

MAJOR: Tim was our best pilot, and Mike, too.

OFFICER: They always kidded each other about being sky hogs.

MUSIC: STINGER CUE. BUILD AND FADE.

FATHER: (FADES IN) And that's all the government could tell us. Guess we won't ever know any more. Yes, it's just like Tim said, it was sort of the minor leagues. He didn't get the Distinguished Flying Cross.

Never given a chance to win an oak leaf cluster. The thing Tim was trying to fight can't be chalked up on the side of a plane.

But the way we like to look at it, it isn't the league that makes the pitcher—and Tim was doing a mighty fine job. Teamwork to the end. He sort of held the fort while the other guys brought back the glory.

Don't many people know about him—guess they never will—but he'll always be our private hero. Families are sort of queer that way. Guess you can understand, if you've ever had a boy, and a fine one!

Well. If you just excuse me for a minute, I'll take

this box on up to the attic. It doesn't help Mom any, to see it sitting around.

SOUND: SLOW, SOFT FOOTSTEPS.

FATHER: (VOICE FADING UNTIL COMPLETLY OFF) But we are sure proud of our Tim, if you know what I mean.

Agnes Eckhardt—Final Exam

# ACKNOWLEDGMENTS

For decades it's been a nonstop refrain from family and fans—I needed to write a book. My response was always, "Are you serious? I'm responsible for two hours of television, five days a week, fifty-two weeks a year. We never get a moment's rest."

Then suddenly in 2012 a bomb dropped. Both my shows were canceled on the same day, victims of the changing world of television, which had splintered from the three-network world of broadcasting into the brave new world of hundreds of channels of cable, streaming, and on-demand. It was a devastating blow and it took me a long time to mourn the loss. For the first time in my life I had the luxury of pausing, but I'm a storyteller and it wasn't long before I dusted off my Dictaphone and began this memoir.

Above all I would like to acknowledge my husband, Bob, and my four children for enriching my life so much and for the sacrifices they made to enable my passion for writing. I especially want to thank Cathy, whose selfless and endless dedication to this book was awesome. Thank you, Cathy, and much love. And thank you also to my son, Bob, for his unfailing encouragement. His clear, unambiguous, concise thinking and his endless hours of work, whether by my side or from across the planet, allowed me to cross the finish line. Much gratitude and love. I am eternally grateful to Robin Volker for transcribing from that secondhand Dictaphone, from the beginning of this memoir and through its earliest stages. Because she was so familiar with this story, she furnished me with a reader's reaction.

It did not take long before I realized how different writing a book is from writing for television. I felt like I was back in school, but just like then, I was somehow blessed with great teachers. Patty Matson guided me to the sharp mind and gentle touch of Michael Carlisle, the extraordinary literary agent who, with his colleague at Inkwell David Forrer, went far above and beyond the call of duty to become full-time coach and cheerleader. Possibly because they were at the end of their wits, they introduced me to Leslie Wells. I hit it off instantly with this smart and engaging fellow southerner and have enjoyed every moment working with her and relished her every editorial comment.

After the first draft was finished I suffered a debilitating stroke, which seriously affected my voice. Many suggested I engage a ghostwriter to step in, but as I was determined to write every word myself, this became quite the relay race and required some seriously committed transcribing assistance. Cindy and Michael of Proof Positive Papers brought their court stenographer skills into play. I send gratitude to my team of health aides—Cora, Pascal, Tiffany, and Carmen—who saw how important this book was to me and jumped in and picked up the dictation baton on top of their other duties.

Also essential to my cheerleading squad were dear friends Tom Murphy, Dominick Nuzzi, Susan Lucci, Helmut Huber, Carole Shure, and Ginger Smith and fellow writers Larry David and Scott Frank. Deep appreciation to my entertainment lawyer, Geoffrey Menin; my business manager, Jack Morris; and my superlative agent, Lou Weiss, who, with his wife, Alice, became a lifelong friend. To Lola I can only say, thank you for being my best friend and helping me always keep my thinking straight.

I could have been knocked over by a feather when I got the news that several publishers wanted my book. They were all so smart that it was a difficult choice, but then came an offer from Matt Inman at Crown. I just loved Matt's knowledge of the broadcast landscape, but it was his polite suggestions on how I could improve a sentence that hooked me. Now that Matt's comments have been checked off, I'm happy to say thank you.

With the manuscript in my editor's hands, I began a task I had been looking forward to: thanking the incredible individuals who made my professional life not just a possibility but a joy. Having only mentioned a few members of our extraordinarily creative company of writers, producers, and crew and cast members in this memoir, I wanted to acknowledge each person who contributed to our close-knit creative family. Each and every one has enriched my life beyond measure.

I had it all worked out. I would do it alphabetically—by show, and then by craft. Thus I would start my list with *All My Children* and then progress through actors, camera operators, carpenters, directors, grips, the hair and makeup teams, my amazing producing team, and finally my beloved roundtable of writers. (Could there be anyone after double *W*s, the peerless Wisner Washam?) My crazy memory would guide me down a lovely trail of gratitude and remembrances that would lead me to *Loving* and then *One Life to Live*.

And so I began. Starting alphabetically with *All My Children,* I listed the following superlative actors who took what we put on the page and brought Pine Valley to life: Judith Barcroft, Julia Barr, Nicholas Benedict, Peter Bergman, Vasili Bogazianos, Kay Campbell, David Canary, Mark Consuelos,

Matthew Cowles, Kim Delaney, Josh Duhamel, Candice Earley, Mary Fickett, Hugh Franklin, Sarah Michelle Gellar, Richard Hatch, Fra Heflin, Eileen Herlie, Vincent Irizarry, Francesca James, Larry Keith, Michael E. Knight . . . But as I came to each name, I started thinking . . . and reminiscing . . . and dictating anecdotes about each person. How Judith infused a delicate vulnerability into Anne . . . how Michael brought Tad to life . . . how Francesca evolved from gifted actress to consummate producer. . . . It was hard to keep in order. And I hadn't even gotten to Ruth Warrick, whose genius creation of Phoebe kept me laughing out loud. Did she really meet with Gorbachev to talk about *All My Children*?

I started to laugh at the realization that I had been delusional to think I could list everyone. Even if I kept my thank-yous to *All My Children, Loving,* and *One Life to Live.* I would be covering more than one hundred years of daytime drama . . . five days a week, fifty-two weeks a year. The acknowledgments would be longer than the memoir!

So I thought the best thing to do would be to share just one story that sums up the shared bond of our company of artists.

It was 2008 and in a corporate cost-cutting move, ABC had announced that *One Life* and *All My Children* production would soon move to Los Angeles from their longtime production studio on West Sixty-Sixth Street. I wanted to make a visit to the set to thank some of the crew who had decided not to relocate to the West Coast and take my youngest grandchildren to see a bit of my world. It was a lovely but bittersweet visit. I was the proud grandma as Bobby, Maggie, and Jack were on their best behavior as we approached the checkout at the cafeteria. As I reached for my wallet a voice behind me forcefully announced, "Drop it, Agnes. Your money's no good here."

Startled, the kids and I turned around to see one of our

burly camera operators stepping up to the cashier with his credit card. I blocked his way with my card. "No way, Jim, I'm buying *you* lunch."

"Agnes, that just ain't gonna happen." Addressing Bobby, Maggie, and Jack, he continued, "I have worked on your grandma's show for thirty-two years. We all love this show and we love working together. We continue to be inspired by your grandma's writing, and we treasure the opportunity to be a part of trying to make this world a kinder place. Kids, your grandma's put my four kids through college. So tell her to drop the credit card."

As I traded my credit card for a hug, everyone in the cafeteria started clapping and hugging one another. And we are family, so to each of my "non-blood" family members, all my thanks and love from the bottom of my heart.

More than anything, though, I'm truly blessed to have such a wonderful family, who remain an essential part of my life. Cathy and Paul live nearby. Their eldest, Kelly, and her husband, Jeff, and beautiful daughter, Emma, live in Atlanta, while Amy works in the New York fashion business. Mary started the New Leaf Club to help youth find alternatives to alcohol and drugs. Her eldest, Ceara, runs the Appalachia School of Holistic Herbalism in Asheville, North Carolina, and helps her daughter, Faye, pursue her career as a youth model. Erin married fellow Georgetown grad Matt Pfeiffer and has brought Riley into the world. Rory and Galen are working on their careers. Bob and Sarah are in DC, engaging unemployed youth in environmental restoration through the Earth Conservation Corps and putting Bobby, Maggie, and Jack to work on many of their documentary films on environmental heroes such as conservationist Dr. Sylvia Earle. Emily lives in New Rochelle and works for the American Folk Art Museum.

Her son, Oliver, lives in Scotland with his wife, Becky, whom he met at St. Andrews. It's almost as if I am living my life with them. With four children, eleven grandchildren, and three great-grandchildren, not a day goes by that I don't appreciate how rich my life is because of them.

I send each of them my love and thanks for their help and patience during all the years I spent living in my real world of make-believe and the writing of this memoir.

## PHOTO INSERT CREDITS

**Page 1:** *(top, bottom left, and bottom right)* Courtesy of the author

**Page 2:** *(top and middle)* Courtesy of the author; *(bottom)* Courtesy of the Priester family

**Page 3:** *(top, middle, and bottom)* Courtesy of the author

**Page 4:** *(top and middle)* Courtesy of the author; *(bottom)* Charles Bonnay/The LIFE Images Collection/Getty Images

**Page 5:** *(top)* Charles Bonnay/The LIFE Images Collection/Getty Images; *(middle and bottom)* ABC Photo Archives/ABC via Getty Images

**Page 6:** *(top)* Charles Bonnay/The LIFE Images Collection/Getty Images; *(middle)* Courtesy of the author; *(bottom)* ABC Photo Archives/ABC via Getty Images

**Page 7:** *(top)* Courtesy of the author; *(middle)* © American Broadcasting Companies, Inc.; *(bottom)* Rick Rowell/ABC via Getty Images

**Page 8:** *(top left)* Ethan Miller/Getty Images Entertainment; *(top right)* Donna Svennevik/ABC Photo Archives/ABC via Getty Images; *(bottom)* Courtesy of the author

# ABOUT THE AUTHOR

Agnes Nixon was a writer and producer, best known for creating the Emmy Award–winning soap operas *All My Children, One Life to Live,* and *Loving.* In 1981 Nixon received the rarely presented Trustees Award from the Academy of Television Arts and Sciences, becoming the first writer and woman to be honored. In 1992, Nixon was inducted into the Television Hall of Fame; in 1994, she became the first female writer to join the Soap Opera Hall of Fame; and in 2010, she received the Lifetime Achievement Award from the Academy of Television Arts and Sciences.